FOREIGN EXCHANGE CRISES

FOREIGN EXCHANGE CRISES

CRISES

An Essay in Economic Pathology

PAUL EINZIG

SECOND EDITION

MACMILLAN
ST MARTIN'S PRESS
1970

First edition 1968
Second edition 1970

Published by
MACMILLAN AND CO LTD
Little Essex Street London W C 2
and also at Bombay Calcutta and Madras
Macmillan South Africa (Publishers) Pty Ltd Johannesburg
The Macmillan Company of Australia Pty Ltd Melbourne
The Macmillan Company of Canada Ltd Toronto
St Martin's Press Inc New York
Gill and Macmillan Ltd Dublin

Library of Congress catalog card no. 68–19638

Printed in Great Britain by
R. & R. CLARK LTD
Edinburgh

CONTENTS

PREFACE TO
THE SECOND EDITION

THE major changes that have occurred since the first edition
of this book was written in 1967 necessitated a drastic revision
of its material. The devaluation of sterling and of the franc,
the adoption of the two-tier gold system, the strengthening of
the dollar as a result of the spectacular increase of American
short-term and long-term borrowing in Europe, and of course
the revaluation of the D. mark, had to be dealt with in order to
bring the book up to date.

The failure of the defence of sterling by means of unlimited
official forward exchange operations has amply confirmed the
warnings I emphatically made in the first edition. I am convinced more firmly than ever that no technical devices, however
ingenious, can by themselves safeguard a country with a
basically weak currency against foreign exchange crises culminating in devaluations, and that nothing short of a national
regeneration could secure us in the long run against the frequent
recurrence of such crises.

The changes in the situation during the last two years have
impelled me to reconsider some opinions I expressed in the
first edition. Two years ago I was firmly opposed to an
increase in the official American price of gold. As a result of
the devaluation of sterling in November 1967, and of the series
of crises that followed it, I now feel that the process of deterioration in the international monetary situation has passed the
point of no return. I have reluctantly come to the conclusion that nothing short of a drastic realignment of gold
parities, involving a major devaluation of the dollar itself,
could restore confidence in the major currencies. An attempt

to restore confidence by means of deflation would call for such drastic deflationary measures that it might initiate a self-aggravating deflationary spiral with incalculable consequences. It might even lead to a series of violent demonstrations causing wholesale destruction of life and property. Unless and until an adequate degree of discipline to ensure the prevention of such irresponsible reactions can be restored, even creeping inflation must be regarded as a smaller evil than the degree of deflation that would be required to check it.

In a review of the first edition of this book, Professor Kenen alleged that it was 'strewn with factual errors'. Having now re-examined the material with extra care, I found no justification for this charge. When challenged about having failed to quote any concrete instances, Professor Kenen merely quoted two instances from a book of over two hundred pages, and both of them were quite obviously mere differences of opinion. But then, conceivably, the Provost of Columbia University is so utterly convinced of his own infallibility that he considers any opinion that differs from his opinion a factual error.

120 CLIFFORD'S INN,   P. E.
LONDON, E.C.4
December 1969

PREFACE TO
THE FIRST EDITION

HAVING described and analysed in more than two scores of
books and in thousands of articles a great many foreign exchange crises over a period of half a century, I now feel the
time has come for summing up my findings and conclusions.
I have done so in the present book, which is an attempt to
diagnose foreign exchange crises in general, ascertain their
causes, prognosticate the likely course of the diseases and examine any possible remedies.

I have followed foreign exchange crises first-hand in the
course of innumerable visits to foreign exchange departments.
I have also made a point of reading a great deal of what others
have written on that subject in several languages. It has always
been my main professional interest and also my favourite hobby
to study foreign exchange crises and to try to predict their outcome. I have got into the bad habit of writing about them with
a display of assurance which I seldom really feel. This confes-
sion, which has been long overdue, is none the less sincere for
being rather belated. In order to express what I truly feel I
could do no better than adapt freely, with apologies to Goethe's
memory, the oft-quoted admission made by his immortal hero,
Faust, in a moment of despair born in that agonising feeling of
frustration with which I am all too familiar :

> I have studied foreign exchange crises,
> Their technique and their history, too,
> And even — alas — their theory,
> With ardent labour through and through.
> Yet here I stand, as wise, poor fool
> As when I first time went to school.

This mistranslation of a superb classical passage from one of the world's literary masterpieces may be a mild exaggeration. But the fact it is intended to convey is that every now and again I feel utterly exasperated, just as Faust must have been, about the limitations of my knowledge — indeed of human knowledge — on a subject to which I have devoted my life. It is true, I have familiarised myself thoroughly with the technical aspects of abnormal foreign exchange movements. I have tried to explore their broader aspects and their psychological causes, and to ascertain their immediate and ultimate effects. I have sought to gain guidance from the experience of the past, covering in my *History of Foreign Exchange* a much longer period than anyone has ever attempted to cover before me.

Yet, like Dr Faust, the more deeply I have tried to penetrate into the mysteries of foreign exchange the more painfully I have come to realise that it is not given to me really to *know*. But unlike him, I could not even delude myself with the idle hope that I might overcome my frustration at the cost of selling my soul to Mephistopheles.

I have long given up hope of ever being able to achieve a full knowledge of the entire range of the relevant facts that are behind any foreign exchange crisis. But even if I could achieve it, it would not necessarily enable me to *know* with any degree of certainty — as distinct from guessing correctly — how the crisis would develop and what effects it would produce. It is true, I can claim that in the past my predictions were correct on many occasions. But in my candid moments I attribute this in a large measure to sheer hunch — or, to use modern language, to extra-sensory perception — rather than to any superior knowledge of the relevant facts or to any superior soundness of my reasoning power in arriving at my conclusions from them.

Tempting as it may be to emulate Faust's reaction to his realisation of the impossibility really to know, I do not propose to follow his example by embarking on a series of exciting but irrelevant adventures and experiences. Instead, I have endeavoured in this book to offer such knowledge as I do possess, inadequate as it is, to those who know even less than I. And to those who know more, or think they do, I suggest with all due diffidence that even they might stand to benefit in some ways by this summing up of the study of a lifetime. After all, my experience, my line of approach and my prejudices are sure to differ from theirs, and it is always useful to approach a subject from a variety of angles.

But whether or not my readers will derive any satisfaction from reading this book, I have derived much satisfaction from writing it, as indeed from my previous writings on foreign exchange. It is a fascinating subject. Although the description of the normal flawless routine of the system may be a dull exercise to all but a handful of specialists — healthy foreign exchanges have no history — the struggle to retain or regain such a dull normal state is full of drama, both tragedy and comedy. To those capable of appreciating this aspect of foreign exchange its crises must surely appear to be more thrilling than a Wimbledon Final and fully as thrilling as an acute political crisis or indeed as a major battle.

My present examination of foreign exchange crises is based largely, though far from exclusively, on the succession of sterling crises in the middle 'sixties. But I did not aim at adding yet another book to the chronologies or inside histories of the sterling crises of 1964–67. I used that interesting experience largely for illustrating my findings on foreign exchange crises in general, while drawing extensively also on evidence provided by many other foreign exchange crises.

Most of the chapters are, I hope, easily understandable to the general reader who possesses the degree of familiarity with foreign exchange that is essential nowadays for the understanding of day-to-day developments which are liable to affect the lives of all of us. But some chapters — especially those on 'Hedging', 'Leads and Lags', 'Supporting of Forward Exchanges' and 'Increasing International Liquidity' — are necessarily technical. My main bid for originality in this book is my attempt to penetrate into the mysteries of Leads and Lags in Chapter 10, and my own proposal of compulsory hedging.

Part of the material in Chapters 9 and 22 was first published in my article appearing in the February 1967 issue of the *Westminster Bank Review*. My thanks are due to its editor for his permission to reproduce it here. I am also indebted, as usual, to the large number of foreign exchange dealers who provided a high proportion of facts and their interpretations contained in this book. My admiration for these nameless heroes of the foreign exchange market increases with each visit I pay to foreign exchange departments.

Although I devoted considerable space to the definition of 'foreign exchange crises' I deemed it outside the scope of the present book to define the various elementary terms employed. For such definitions I must refer the reader to my *Textbook on Foreign Exchange*. Those interested in the more technical chapters will find more detailed treatment of the subject in the recently published second edition of my *Dynamic Theory of Forward Exchange*.

120 CLIFFORD'S INN,   P. E.
LONDON, E.C.4
September 1967

CHAPTER ONE

INTRODUCTORY

DOES Schopenhauer's pessimistic philosophy, according to which happiness is a negative notion because it simply means absence of unhappiness, apply to foreign exchange? Is stability of exchanges merely an abnormal absence of instability which is really the normal state of affairs? Such is the impression that is conveyed, albeit unwittingly, by books on monetary history and by daily financial comments alike. We who live in a period when acute foreign exchange crises follow each other in close succession may find it strange to come across references to foreign exchange crises in books and articles during the stable decades that preceded the first World War. By comparison with our own experience the foreign exchange situation of that period must appear to us happy and uneventful in retrospect. But those who lived during that period must have found their relatively simple foreign exchange problems almost as perturbing as we now find our incomparably graver difficulties.

The history of currency appears to be a record of foreign exchange crises or of narrowly averted foreign exchange crises. It is the chronicle of successful or unsuccessful attacks on various exchanges, of devaluations and (much less frequently) revaluations, of wild fluctuations of exchange rates, of successful or unsuccessful attempts at stabilisation, and of hard struggles to maintain stability once achieved. Yet there have also been many periods of stable and uneventful exchanges in between crises.

Literature on foreign exchange devotes much less space to such stable periods. It is not as if they were less important than crises to those interested in foreign exchange. After all, the aim of human wisdom as applied to foreign exchange policy is to ensure a normal functioning of the system. But since such

periods are uneventful they are less interesting than the excite-
ment caused by instability or threat of instability.

Exchange movements of a purely technical character, or even
slightly wider movements caused by seasonal or other normal
influences, are of interest only to those directly concerned in
practice with foreign exchange transactions, and to specialists
writing textbooks about them. The wider public only becomes
interested when there is instability or acute threat of instability.
But even experts pay much less attention to exchanges during
happy uneventful periods. They may produce occasional
textbooks, or brief routine paragraphs covering the previous
day's foreign exchange market. But the output is quite negligible compared with the literature that springs up under the
influence of disturbed conditions. The more chaotic the exchanges are the more books and articles are published on them.

For instance, the great recoinage in the 1690s gave rise to a
flood of literature on foreign exchange. In the light of the
immediate problems and controversies the more basic problems also come under much closer scrutiny than during stable
periods. There was a boom in the literature on foreign
exchange during the Napoleonic Wars, and of course also
during and after the two World Wars. Each crisis had something to teach those who experienced it and also subsequent
generations. Crises were invariably accompanied by lively
controversies which led to a more penetrating analysis of the
functioning of the foreign exchange system.

Our first task is to try to define what we mean by a foreign
exchange crisis. It is a very difficult task, and it is very
tempting to take an easy way out by quoting, as an excuse of
our inability to produce an acceptable definition, the familiar
witticism that we may not be able to define an elephant and
yet we recognise one when we see one. Unfortunately this
would not do. While an elephant is always easily recognisable
a foreign exchange crisis is not. Its symptoms are often not
self-explanatory and they are largely a matter of degree.
Indeed in recent experience the presence of a foreign exchange
crisis was at times successfully disguised, and was only admitted

after it was over. Moreover, it is a matter of opinion whether suppressed crises should be classified among crises.

According to the *Oxford Dictionary* the term 'crisis' implies a 'period of danger or suspense' that is supposed to be, by definition, of brief duration. But we have experienced prolonged crises in the course of which a series of climaxes alternated with relatively calm intervals and even with spells of recoveries. The crisis of the 'thirties belonged to that category, although it is possible to argue that it was a chronic depression punctuated by acute crises. This is, of course, a matter of definition.

An even better example was provided by the sterling crisis which began in November 1964 and continued with intervals throughout 1965, 1966, 1967, 1968 and 1969. Sterling was in crisis throughout that period, with several climaxes when there were acute runs on the pound.

It was in this sense of prolonged crisis that André Siegfried gave his famous book on Britain in 1930 the title of *England's Crisis*. (Note the singular.) In the same sense a symposium on the dollar's difficulties in the early 'sixties, edited by Seymour E. Harris, was called *The Dollar in Crisis*. My own book on the frequently recurrent difficulties of France and of the franc during the middle 'thirties was named *France's Crisis* (with apologies to André Siegfried). From these instances it is evident that prolonged or frequently recurring acute difficulties may come under the definition of a crisis, even though it is arguable that it is a series of crises with intervals between them.

Although heavy and persistent buying pressure as well as selling pressure on an exchange can upset the equilibrium and can cause grave inconvenience, it does not come under the definition of a crisis. An *embarras de richesse* can always be dealt with effectively if it is tackled firmly in the right way. Only heavy selling pressure may produce a crisis. But then one exchange's buying pressure is another's selling pressure.

If selling pressure is on such a scale as to endanger the stability of a fixed exchange, forcing the Government eventually to abandon its existing fixed parity, we are obviously in the presence of a foreign exchange crisis. But if the parity is flexible — that is, it is subject to frequent adjustments — its adjustment under selling pressure need not necessarily be considered a crisis. And if the system in operation is that of floating exchange rates — under which exchanges are allowed to find their level — then selling pressure that causes the exchange to depreciate need not be considered a crisis unless the extent of its depreciation is definitely in excess of what the authorities regard as the admissible limits of its fluctuations. So the degree of selling pressure which is high enough to come under the definition of a crisis depends on the foreign exchange system in operation.

It is a matter of opinion whether even heavy selling pressure on an exchange which is adequately and more than adequately backed by a strong reserve must be considered a crisis. In 1961 when *The Dollar in Crisis* was published, the American gold reserve was certainly fully adequate and there was no real danger of its decline below danger level in the near future. Nevertheless, the name chosen for the book was not a misnomer, for there were from time to time acute dollar scares and their aggravation might have depleted the gold reserve to an alarming extent. And it is in any case arguable that selling pressure which reduces the reserve to a level at which it is still sufficient to maintain stability but at which the technical strength of the exchange is no longer deemed to be impregnable comes within the definition of a crisis.

On the other hand, if the selling pressure merely brings about a long-overdue redistribution of gold and corrects a chronic maldistribution it need not be considered a crisis. It rather depends on the point of view from which the movement is looked upon.

Yet another question is whether selling pressure which is met without any spectacular decline of the gold reserve, through realisations of foreign assets or through the borrowing of foreign long-term capital, should be considered a crisis. In such situations there is no evidence of a crisis, because the symptoms are suppressed as a result of changes in the international capital situation of the country concerned. The exchange rates do not move against the national currency, nor is there any strong one-sided trend in the foreign exchange market. Nevertheless, the situation is far from being normal and healthy. Even if the authorities of the country concerned pretend that there is nothing amiss, a trend which results in the liquidation of a considerable part of a country's external reserves represented by its accumulated long-term assets abroad, or which transfers vital national assets into foreign ownership or burdens the country with a heavy foreign debt, may be considered to amount to a suppressed crisis.

Another insidious form of crisis is a situation in which selling pressure is met with the aid of contracting foreign short-term liabilities or, worst of all, with the aid of official selling of foreign exchange for forward delivery. Such crises are apt to be even more effectively camouflaged than the realisation of foreign assets or the transfer of domestic assets into foreign hands. On more than one occasion during 1964–67 when selling pressure on sterling was met by such means the impression was conveyed that the crisis was thereby solved. Yet in truth it was merely temporarily concealed. But in spite of this the credit arrangements inspired confidence on each occasion and caused a recovery of sterling, because the foreign exchange market's primary interest lies in the immediate position which is well safeguarded with the aid of such arrangements.

Having regard to all the above considerations it is permissible to suggest that heavy one-sided selling pressure on an exchange, which tends to have self-aggravating effect and which necessitates the adoption of drastic defensive measures in order to maintain stability, comes under the definition of a crisis. In the following chapters an attempt is made to examine the causes of foreign exchange crises. To say that a foreign exchange crisis is the result of one-sided selling pressure is of course like saying that death is due to heart failure. It is technically true but it does not by itself really explain anything. Those investigating an unexplained death will want to know what caused the heart failure. And those inquiring into the causes of a foreign exchange crisis want, of course, to ascertain the causes responsible for the selling pressure.

When investigating these causes we have to distinguish between immediate causes and more remote causes. The latter again may be causes just once removed or causes several times removed. If a surplus of imports over exports is the immediate cause of a selling pressure it may be due to excessive imports caused by increased domestic purchasing power, which again may be the result of a set of direct or indirect causes making for inflation.

It will be seen that a foreign exchange crisis can be due to an almost infinite variety of direct or indirect causes. Indeed hardly anything of importance can happen in the economic, political or social system of a country that would not tend to react directly or indirectly on its exchange rate through increasing or reducing buying or selling pressure. Influences that are liable to affect the foreign exchange market abnormally are at work all the time, and the tendency of the exchange rate is the result of the balance between favourable and unfavourable influences. Nor do all such influences originate in the country concerned. Exchange rates are necessarily influenced by developments abroad which affect the currency of the foreign country concerned, thereby affecting the relative value of the two currencies.

The main direct causes of selling pressure on an exchange are as follows :

(1) Decline of visible or invisible exports.
(2) Increase of visible or invisible imports.
(3) Adverse change in the terms of trade.
(4) Increased leads in respect of payments made for imports.
(5) Increased lags in respect of payments received for exports.
(6) Increased Government spending abroad.
(7) Excessive capital exports.
(8) Repatriation or withdrawal of foreign capital.

(9) Repayment of foreign debts.
(10) Withdrawal of foreign balances.
(11) Flight of domestic capital.
(12) Pure speculative selling.
(13) Hedging.
(14) Outward Interest Arbitrage.

When it comes to indirect causes it would be idle to try to compile a list that could be claimed to be comprehensive. The scope of Part II, dealing with indirect causes, is confined to some of the most important among them.

Finally, an attempt is made in Part III to examine the various measures adopted or proposed to meet foreign exchange crises, whether they aim at camouflaging the crisis or resisting it or abandoning resistance to it.

CHAPTER TWO

SYMPTOMS OF CRISES

IT is as important to be able to ascertain at an early stage the causes of foreign exchange crises as it is to diagnose an illness at an early stage, because the choice of remedies depends in both instances on the cause of the trouble and the delay in their application is bound to aggravate the trouble. Unfortunately the symptoms of foreign exchange crises are usually very much alike no matter what the cause may be. What is worse, many of the symptoms are present even in more or less normal conditions, and the difference between them and crisis-symptoms is merely a matter of degree.

The following are the principal symptoms of foreign exchange crises :

(1) Selling pressure on the spot exchange.

(2) Selling pressure on the forward exchange.

(3) Increase of the turnover in the foreign exchange market.

(4) Alternatively, a large volume of inquiry but reluctance of dealers to commit themselves to actual operations.

(5) Increased turnover in forward transactions for very short dates.

(6) Increased turnover in 'value today' or 'value to-morrow' spot transactions.

(7) Increased turnover in very short Euro-currency or other loans.

(8) Depreciating tendency of the exchange rates under the pressure of excess of selling orders seeking counterpart.

(9) Depreciating tendency of exchange rates through adjustments of quotations even in the absence of a change in supply–demand relationship.

(10) Development of a one-way market.

(11) Development of a disorderly self-aggravating market.

(12) Rise in interest rates, especially for short maturities.

(13) Rise in the dollar price of gold in the free market.

(14) Reduction of foreign bank balances.

(15) Increase in forward covering of such balances and of other balances owned by non-residents.

(16) Increase of forward covering of commercial claims or liabilities.

(17) Hedging against depreciation of foreign investments.

(18) Increase of leads by importers anxious to cover well in advance their payments in terms of foreign currencies.

(19) Increase of leads by foreign exporters anxious to dispose of their claims for goods invoiced in the importers' currency.

(20) Increase of lags by exporters anxious to defer the realisation of the proceeds of sales invoiced in foreign currencies.

(21) Increase of lags by foreign importers anxious to maintain their liabilities for goods invoiced in the exporters' currency.

(22) Speeding up imports.

(23) Deferring exports.

(24) Slow-down of the market mechanism in adjusting disequilibrium between supply–demand and rates.

(25) Nervous market in which rates respond to transactions to an extent that is out of proportion to the amounts involved.

(26) Receptivity of the market to rumours.

(27) An undertone of pessimism amidst which every development is given an unfavourable interpretation.

(28) Panicky selling.

(29) Widening of margins between buying and selling quotations.

(30) Widening of discrepancies between rates quoted simultaneously in various markets, and even in the same market.

(31) Widening of discrepancies between forward rates for various maturities.

(32) Widening of profit margins on interest arbitrage.

(33) In case of intervention, the authorities become virtually the sole providers of counterparts.

(34) In the absence of intervention the rates move until they have depreciated sufficiently to attract counterparts.

(35) Difficulty in dealing in broken amounts.

(36) Difficulty in dealing for odd dates.

The extent of selling pressure need not in itself determine whether the market is normal or not. Exchanges are liable to become subject to strong selling pressure through seasonal and other normal influences, or through the fortuitous coincidence of a number of substantial normal transactions. A single large and urgent order reaching a lifeless market which does not provide a counterpart immediately might convey the impression of the beginnings of abnormal pressure. Yet a counterpart might be forthcoming in due course and the market would then resume its previous condition.

Before the forward market developed properly all the abnormal selling pressure was on the spot rate. Today it is divided between spot and forward, as indeed it has to be because the two markets merge into each other and pressure on the one soon spreads on the other. On particularly hectic days, when rates are expected to move materially during the market hours of the same day, speculative transactions are apt to be concentrated mainly on spot exchanges because dealers expect to be able to close their positions and to take their profits on the same day. On the other hand, when the changes in the rates are not expected to be quite so imminent most speculative pressure is on forward rates, because many sellers do not possess the exchanges they want to sell and have no wish to be placed in a position to have to buy them within the two days at the end of which spot exchanges have to be delivered.

The increase in the turnover in spot exchanges for 'value today' or 'value tomorrow' — which means delivery on the same day or on the following day instead of in two days — means that there is much speculation by means of selling spot terms of the national currency by foreign banks is one of the familiar symptoms of a crisis. Such holdings are apt to become reduced for other reasons — such as a current balance of payments surplus or a net import of long-term capital, or the withdrawal of gold where this is possible — and the incidence of normal transactions is also apt to produce that effect. But whenever there is a crisis in the air foreign banks and their customers tend to reduce to the indispensable minimum their working balances in the threatened currency. Alternatively they cover hitherto uncovered balances, in which case the total of the balances remains unchanged and pressure on the exchange assumes the form of selling forward exchanges.

In a normal market the foreign balances that are sold usually find other foreign buyers, in which case the totals remain unchanged even though a high proportion of them has changed hands. When the authorities intervene in support of the market they buy the balances sold by private holders, so that the net private foreign holdings become reduced. Alternatively they support the forward rate at a level at which inward interest arbitrage becomes profitable, in which case the net result is that the balances sold by their original holders are acquired by arbitrageurs. Even if the grand total of foreign balances remains more or less unchanged individual banks are apt to lose large amounts through the incidence of operations. It is always risky, therefore, to rely on the limited experience of a single bank, or of a small number of banks, when forming an opinion about the trend of foreign balances. Official statistics published by the leading countries are the only dependable guide. In the case of Britain they appear only each quarter, and by the time they appear they are apt to be out of date.

Increased covering and hedging is one of the obvious crisis symptoms. In the London market considerable importance is attached to evidence of hedging by the 'Great West Road' (an industrial district near London where many American branch factories are situated) because when foreign holders of U.K. direct investments deem it necessary to insure themselves against a devaluation of sterling it usually indicates a sterling scare. But covering and hedging may also occur in trades with narrow profit margins when the prospective depreciation is not expected to go beyond existing support points.

Likewise, even the anticipation of normal movements within support points is liable to cause a slight lengthening of leads and lags, especially in respect of staple products on which the profit margin is narrow. But it is only when a currency becomes devaluation-prone or revaluation-prone that changes in the length of leads and lags become strongly evident. Bankers notice that their customers change their usual financial arrangements in order to cover earlier their purchases of foreign exchanges and to defer the sale of the proceeds of their exports. This symptom is not evident in the market itself, but banks with a wide commercial clientele are only too familiar with it. There is even a tendency for changing the timing, not only of payments arising from imports and exports but imports and exports themselves.

Reference was made earlier to the tendency towards self-adjustment of discrepancies between supply and demand through adjustment of prices. Occasionally such self-adjustment is strangely deficient. Although no counterpart is forthcoming at the rates quoted, most dealers are unwilling to adjust their quotations to a sufficient extent to attract a counterpart. Such situations occur when expectations by various dealers differ sharply, or when most dealers prefer to sit on the fence.

One of the early symptoms of a crisis — a symptom which is liable to recur also at later stages — is an atmosphere of nervousness in which dealers are very much on the lookout for some pointer and are inclined to attach exaggerated importance to any minor buying or selling pressure. Such a phase is liable to be reached when after a relatively wide movement the rates have reached a state of uneasy equilibrium from which they are liable to depart at the slightest pressure in either direction.

In such a situation dealers are inclined to seize upon news items or rumours of small importance which they would probably disregard in situations when the market has a definite trend or in which it appears to be steady. Any such reports or rumours are liable to cause a movement of the rates.

There are days and even periods when the market has a distinct undertone of pessimism and interprets every development in a sense unfavourable to the exchange under pressure. Thus even measures adopted in defence of the exchange — such as an increase of the Bank rate, for instance — are interpreted as panic-measures or as the Government's last throw before submitting to the inevitable necessity to devalue. In the absence of full information about the amount of the gold and foreign exchange reserve the market's estimates of the losses incurred in the course of the official support of the exchange are apt to be grossly exaggerated. Likewise pessimistic forecasts about the trade figures whose publication is imminent gain acceptance. This attitude is liable to culminate in large-scale selling in a panicky spirit.

Technically, a widening of margins between buying and selling quotations is a crisis-symptom. As is well known, dealers, in order not to disclose prematurely whether they are buyers or sellers, quote both buying and selling rates at which they are prepared to deal in standard amounts either way, provided that the rate is accepted immediately. When the market is steady the spread between the two rates is apt to be narrow, but when the market is uneasy dealers want to safeguard themselves by quoting wide spreads in case the rate should move even during the seconds between the quotation of the rate and its acceptance. Likewise, discrepancies between rates quoted simultaneously in various markets also widen, partly because of more irregular movements in all markets and partly because dealers are too busy to find much time for arbitrage in space. For the same reason, discrepancies are liable to develop even between quotations in the same market. Departures of forward rates from their 'equilibrium line' — i.e., interest parities for various maturities — are likely to become more pronounced. If forward rates are free they are inclined to deviate from their interest parities to a considerable extent, until the discrepancy attracts interest arbitrage within the limits of funds available for that purpose. Those limits are apt to be wider as a result of the development of Euro-currency markets, but prolonged one-sided operations are apt to reduce them.

One of the symptoms is the disproportionate widening of the discount on the forward exchange for very short maturities and on very short Euro-currency deposits. Speculators are prepared to pay fantastically high rates per annum for forward exchanges or Euro-currencies, especially over week-ends, during periods when an early devaluation is widely expected. This is largely because most devaluations since the last war were announced during week-ends. Short rates are subjected to pressure also on the eve of IMF annual meetings, in anticipation of decisions to adjust parities or support points.

Yet another symptom is that in hectic dealings it becomes more difficult to deal in broken amounts or for odd dates. Most dealers are too busy to be bothered with figures other than the standard amounts for transactions or their multiple, or with forward maturities other than the standard dates 1, 2, 3, 6 and 12 months.

Even the most experienced dealer cannot claim to be certain whether any of the above symptoms indicate the presence or the approach of a crisis until the symptoms become very obvious and very advanced. In the earlier stages large but not abnormal operations are liable to be mistaken for the beginnings of a crisis. The task of the authorities in deciding whether the situation calls for intervention is far from easy.

PART ONE

CAUSES OF CRISES

CHAPTER THREE

IMPORT SURPLUS CRISES

ONE of the first rules one learns about foreign exchange is that trends of exchange rates are supposed to be determined by trends of foreign trade — an export surplus means a firm exchange and an import surplus means a weak exchange. On the basis of this popular rule, whenever an exchange is weak it is widely assumed that there is an import surplus behind its weakness. As there is inevitably a time-lag between goods movements through the Customs and the publication of the relevant statistics it may take weeks before it can be ascertained whether the assumption was correct. Moreover, changes in leads and lags vitiate the immediate effect of the trade balance on exchange rates. But in a remarkably large proportion of instances the assumption proved to be broadly correct. This in spite of the fact that, like most elementary rules, the rule concerning the effect of import–export relationship and exchange rate trends is grossly oversimplified.

On many occasions the adverse trend of the exchanges was sought to be explained on the grounds of activities by the wicked 'gnomes' — always a popular line. But when the trade figures came to be published it was usually found that, even if the gnomes had not existed at all, the exchanges would have behaved substantially as they had, because their depreciation was amply justified by a recent trade deficit. All the gnomes had probably done was to reinforce the adverse pressure on the exchange, by carrying out transactions fully justified by the natural weakness generated by the import surplus.

Admittedly, the trade balance explanation is apt to be even more often correct, and it is apt to be correct to an even higher degree if, instead of being applied in its unsophisticated

form, the main complicating elements are taken into consideration.

(1) It is not changes in the volume of imports and exports
that matter from the point of view of the exchanges but
changes in their value. If the relative volume and composition
of imports and exports remained unchanged but the total value
of exports declined or the total value of imports increased owing
to changes in the prices of goods that entered into foreign trade,
if export prices failed to rise to the same extent as import prices,
or if export prices declined to a larger degree than import
prices, the effect is the same as that of a fall in the volume of
exports or a rise in the volume of imports.

(2) Invisible current items must be taken into consideration.
It is a matter of indifference from the point of view of the effect
of imports and exports on exchanges whether or not they are
recorded by the Customs authorities. Thus an increase in
smuggling has the same effect on the exchange as an increase
in legitimate imports. Because official and on the whole reliable statistics are published about recorded visible trade while
the totals of most invisible trade items are a matter of largely
arbitrary estimates bordering at times on sheer guesswork, the
former commands more prestige. Yet the importance of
changes in invisible imports or exports is often comparable
with that of changes in visible trade.

There are sets of causes liable to affect each invisible export
or import item. Thus countries depending on tourist traffic
for balancing their trade are exposed to foreign exchange crises
by any development liable to deter visitors — bad weather,
major disasters, infectious diseases, unfavourable publicity
about conditions of comfort, travelling facilities, sanitation,
the inhabitants' attitude towards visitors, etc., war or civil
war or threat of war or civil war, major strikes, changes of
fashion in the choice of holiday resorts, tightening of exchange controls, widespread economic depression abroad, etc.

Income from overseas investment is liable to decline through
reductions of dividends owing to bad trade, exchange control
holding up remittances of dividends or interest payments,

drastic local taxation, labour troubles, etc. Income from shipping might decline through a depression in the freight market,
competition of rival merchant fleets, inadequate replacement
of obsolete ships, etc. Income from insurance might fall
through heavy losses on overseas policies, decline in new business, etc. Income from emigrants' remittances is apt to
fluctuate with the ups and downs of employment abroad. It
declines after a decline in new emigration.

Invisible imports are liable to increase through an increase
in travelling abroad, in the use of foreign ships or insurance
companies, through an increase in immigrants' remittances
resulting from an influx of foreign labour, through a net excess
of payments abroad on insurance policies over premium incomes, through an increase in interest and dividends on foreign
capital invested in the country, through increased repatriations
of undistributed profits on such capital, etc.

(3) As far as sterling is concerned, the visible and invisible
trade of the U.K. is not alone in determining current balance
of payments influences. The trade of the Outer Sterling Area,
too, must be taken into consideration. Residents of Sterling
Area countries draw on their sterling balances to meet their
requirements, and official sterling holdings of these countries
can be withdrawn. Although the arrangement made in 1968,
under which official Sterling Area balances are guaranteed,
has reduced withdrawals through distrust in sterling, adverse
balances have to be met out of the sterling reserves.

(4) The terms of payment of imports and exports are an
important influence affecting exchanges. Some goods are paid
for in advance, others on delivery, while others again are
bought and sold on a credit basis. Such credits are usually
short-term — 3 or 6 months — but sometimes medium- and
long-term credits are granted. From the point of view of the
effect of foreign trade transactions on the exchange it is not
the time of placing the order or of the delivery of the goods
that matters but the time when the payment actually leads to
the purchase of the exporter's currency by the importer or the
sale of the importer's currency by the exporter.

B

While payment for consumer goods and raw materials is usually on a short-term credit basis, capital goods are sold on a medium- or long-term credit basis. The exchanges of the exporting country and of the importing country may not be affected by such transactions for years. As we shall see in Chapter 10, even in respect of goods sold against short-term credit the time at which the exchanges are affected depends on whether the transaction is covered by a spot or a short or long forward operation, whether it is financed by banks in the exporting or importing country or in a third country, and whether it is financed in terms of the exporters' currency or the importers' currency or some third currency. Moreover, even after importers have paid for their goods bought from some country with a devaluation-prone currency they are liable to hedge by selling forward the exporting country's currency so long as they have inventories in the goods that are liable to be affected by a devaluation. This is not permitted in the U.K.

(5) Finally, capital transactions are liable to reinforce or counteract the effect of the current trade balance on exchanges. For instance, when a British firm establishes a branch factory abroad and exports the necessary equipment it will figure in the export statistics, but it will not contribute directly and immediately towards increasing buying pressure or mitigating selling pressure on sterling. If the subsidiary firm's capital is transferred in cash instead of in the form of equipment the transaction increases selling pressure on sterling. At a later stage sterling stands to benefit to the extent of dividend payments, transfers of undistributed profits and repatriations of capital. More will be said about this in Chapter 5.

Allowing for current trade balance and capital imports and exports, there is bound to remain a balance in the form of a surplus or a deficit. It is true, even this balance is bound to be offset in some way or other, unless debtors default on their liabilities. According to a conception that was fashionable in the early years after the first World War, the balance of payments is bound to balance and therefore it cannot affect the exchange rate. But it is the process by which the balance of payments balances that is liable to affect exchange rates. If a country has a large import surplus the depreciation of its exchange caused by it may attract buyers who are willing to hold balances or investments in terms of its currency.

Having made all these reservations it is necessary to emphasise that, in spite of them, by and large the crude trade surplus or deficit does tend to affect the exchanges considerably. Much more often than not it does explain the depreciation of the exchange to a large degree. Broadly speaking it is true that a pronounced and persistent weakness of an exchange under heavy pressure is very frequently the result of a large and persistent adverse trade balance. No amount of sophisticated refinements and scholarly reservations alters the basic fact that over-importing is bad for exchanges. When an exchange crisis develops the first question is, therefore — are we importing too much? Or are we exporting too little to pay for our imports?

If trade figures are adverse and the exchange is not weak it may mean that the foreign exchange employed for payment has been acquired earlier, by forward covering for instance; or that payment is not due till later; or that it is being financed for the time being in the exporting country or in some other foreign country or with the aid of borrowed Euro-currency deposits; or that invisible items are in favour of the currency concerned; or that capital transactions are in its favour. Possibly the adverse balance had already produced its effect if imports had been covered in advance, or it will produce its effect later if imports are not payable until later. Conversely, when trade figures or even balance of payments figures show no substantial deficit and the exchange is weak nevertheless, the cause of its weakness usually lies in adverse capital movements, or in a lengthening of leads and lags, or in other effects of distrust in the currency.

Seasonal adverse balance need not cause a crisis, unless the exchange position is so delicately balanced that even an otherwise normal trend is capable of upsetting its balance. Business cycles affect exports and imports considerably and are liable to bring about an intractable adverse balance which would generate a crisis. If prosperity at home means excessive consumption or investment or excessive imports of raw materials, semi-products, capital equipment or consumer goods it could lead to exchange crises — as it did in Britain in a number of instances in the 'fifties and the 'sixties.

However, an unfavourable exchange does not prove the existence of adverse balance any more than does an adverse balance cause necessarily an adverse exchange. High temperature of a patient may be a symptom of scores of illnesses other than influenza, and influenza may be diagnosed on the basis of many symptoms other than high temperature. Economics is no more an exact science than medicine. Even so, when an exchange is weak, unless there is some alternative explanation it is advisable to envisage the possibility that its weakness is due to adverse balance.

But an adverse balance, though a frequent cause of exchange weakness that is developing into crisis, is itself but a symptom indicating deeper-lying causes. It is necessary to find the more fundamental cause in order to form an idea of its likely duration and intensity and to prescribe the appropriate medicine. If it is due, for instance, to a major strike its duration is bound to be limited, even though the interruption of exports might divert foreign purchases to other countries and might cause, therefore, a permanent loss of foreign markets. If the deterioration of the trade balance is due to structural changes its correction is apt to be even more difficult than if it were due to an inflationary overload on the economy.

A deficit, in order to cause a crisis, must be very substantial or very persistent. But the effect of even a relatively moderate deficit is liable to be aggravated by speculation, etc. On the other hand, so long as trade is balanced or at any rate the deficit is well under control the other influences do not very often cause crises. A deficit is frequently at the bottom of crises. For this reason it is always tempting to assume that it is the sole cause and to deal with the crisis on that assumption.

A trade deficit may affect the forward rate in the first instance, especially if it is predictable, through leading to advance covering of a larger volume of imports. That in turn reacts on the spot rate. It is exaggerated by pessimism if it is suspected to be more than seasonal. It is by far the most dangerous immediate cause of the crisis. Speculation, arbitrage and hedging are relatively easily reversible. Any short positions — whether created through pure speculation or through hedging or through longer leads and lags — is a potential source of strength because sooner or later it is liable to become reversed. On the other hand, a trade deficit is a dead loss: it leads to a depletion of the reserve and to the mounting up of external short-term liabilities which have to be met sooner or later. Moreover, it is much slower to react to monetary policy measures than are other direct causes of a crisis. It is therefore no wonder a deficit is more likely to generate pessimism about distant prospects than any other cause except a flight of the national capital.

An exchange crisis caused by speculation, hedging, withdrawal of foreign balances, outflow of funds through interest arbitrage, or lengthening of leads and lags may be dealt with by obtaining foreign support in some form, provided that the support is on an adequate scale and its continuity inspires confidence. To try to deal with an exchange crisis caused by a trade deficit by means of foreign credits, swap arrangements, or drawing rights is, however, a fatal mistake. Its only justification would be if it is employed purely temporarily as a stopgap measure pending the adoption of measures to deal with the causes of the deficit. We must bear in mind that to draw on International Monetary Fund facilities or to secure foreign Central Bank swap facilities or credits, or to make use of SDRs, does not deal with the basic causes which will continue to affect imports and exports. Even the largest IMF drawing rights or Central Bank facilities are bound to become exhausted eventually as a result of a perennial deficit, and possibly the patience of the creditors might become exhausted if there is no evidence that their debtor is prepared to adopt measures to balance his international accounts.

The group of Central Banks which granted support to Britain in November 1964 and on a number of subsequent occasions laid down the rule, when renewing the arrangement in June 1966, that the credits were to be used for the specific purpose of covering withdrawals of foreign balances, and not for covering deficits. The rule is theoretically sound, but in practice it means little. Sterling had to be supported against adverse pressure, irrespective of its causes. By the summer of 1966 the British authorities had no net gold or dollar reserve, for the outstanding amount of their short-term liabilities to the IMF and to foreign Central Banks exceeded the amount of their gold and dollar holdings, even without allowing for the contingent liabilities represented by the dollars sold by the Bank of England for forward delivery. Whenever there was a demand for dollars in excess of supply from private sources, the Bank of England had to cover the deficiency if it wanted to prevent a depreciation of sterling, regardless of whether the demand originated from the withdrawal of balances or from trade deficit or from other causes. Indeed the Bank of England was not even in a position to know what the demand for dollars represented. While banks may ask their non-banking clients for explanation, no questions are ever asked in the foreign exchange market itself. Not until the Bank receives the weekly returns from the U.K. banks can it form an idea whether or not its sales of dollars had served the purpose of covering withdrawals of foreign balances.

If it was wrong to cover a deficit by short-term borrowing, it was even more wrong to cover it by means of official forward exchange operations. The basic causes of the trade balance deficit were unaffected even if its effect on the exchanges was temporarily disguised. Indeed, in given situations to be discussed in a later chapter, they were even aggravated as a result of maintaining the forward exchange at an artificially overvalued level.

Nor is it possible to solve the foreign exchange crisis, except temporarily, through reducing the deficit by means of import surcharges, quotas, embargoes or import deposits. They do not deal with the basic causes of the deficit, indeed they even tend to accentuate the disequilibrium that causes the adverse balance. The same is true about the reinforcement of exchange control which merely enables the country to inflate with impunity as far as the effect on the exchange rates and on the reserves is concerned, at any rate in the short run.

If the deficit is due to excessive domestic demand it must be dealt with by a drastic reduction of that demand. Any attempt at dealing with it in other ways is sheer self-deception that carries its own punishment in the long run. If it is due to deflation abroad then it is for the Government to decide whether to safeguard the parities by means of sympathetic deflation or whether to safeguard the country from imported deflation by means of adjusting its exchange parities to the changed purchasing power parities. Much depends on whether the production system of the country concerned is employed to capacity, also whether there is an international buyers' market or a sellers' market.

If the deficit is due to structural changes, or to the requirements of reconstruction after the devastations of a war or some other form of major disaster, then there is every justification to seek to finance it by means of borrowing abroad, preferably in the form of long-term borrowing pending the adjustment of the economy. The same is true about developing countries which are liable to have a perennial adverse balance.

Of course the ideal solution of a foreign exchange crisis caused by a trade deficit is to eliminate that deficit by means of increasing exports. But I shall try to show in Chapter 19 that this is only practicable in economies which have no inflated consumer demand and which are not employed to capacity. Otherwise the diversion of goods to export trade would leave domestic demand unsatisfied, and since the purchasing power is there it will be employed on increased imports. This occurred much of the time in Britain during 1964–1968. Exports were stimulated by Government-guaranteed long-term credits for the purchase of ships and other capital goods. As a result, delivery dates became even longer and more uncertain, so that British firms had to place their orders abroad. And since they paid cash the net result of the export drive was an aggravation of the pressure on sterling. More will be said about this in Chapter 19.

Britain's experience in 1968 made it clear that under conditions of high employment and creeping inflation it is impossible to defend even a devalued currency without measures to cut home consumption. A devaluation by 14 per cent gave Britain every chance to restore the balance of payments. Exports did increase, but so did imports. Home demand expanded and the vacuum created in supply as a result of higher exports was filled by increased imports. Measures adopted to reduce home demand were highly inadequate, and their effect was more than wiped out by the inexplicable, ill-advised announcement of the Chancellor of the Exchequer that he intended to adopt drastic increases of taxation. The resulting pre-Budget spending spree discredited sterling to such an extent that it continued even after the tax increases. That is why the British devaluation of 1967 was for nearly two years an unmitigated failure. It did not save sterling from repeated import surplus crises during 1968–69. Not until the second half of 1969 was there any improvement, and even this was attributable to the expansion of world trade and to the rise in prices in the United States rather than to a delayed effect of the devaluation.

CHAPTER FOUR

GOVERNMENT
OVERSPENDING ABROAD

THE effect of Government spending abroad on exchanges had already been known in the 16th century, according to evidence contained in Sir Thomas Gresham's dispatches from Antwerp. Purchases of munition on the Continent and repayment of earlier external borrowing made Gresham's task of maintaining the exchange rather difficult from time to time. The chronic weakness of the Spanish maravedi during the same century, in spite of the heavy inflow of gold and silver from the American colonies, was mainly due to heavy expenditure of the armies of Philip II abroad. In the Napoleonic Wars Britain's foreign exchange difficulties were due as much to the cost of wars overseas and subsidies to continental allies as to domestic inflation. The decisive defeat of the Coalition at Austerlitz in 1805 was followed by a recovery of sterling, because it obviated the necessity of continuing the subsidies.

During the two World Wars the effect of Government spending abroad was neutralised, more or less, by inter-Allied loans offsetting the cost of Government expenditure overseas. Even during the early period after the second World War the proceeds of the U.S. loan to Britain, Marshall aid and other forms of American military and economic aid went a long way towards neutralising the natural effect of spending abroad by the British Government. In any case most exchanges remained more or less under control. As for the unprecedented amounts of U.S. Government expenditure on foreign bases and on foreign aid, the U.S. could easily afford them until the late 'fifties, thanks to the perennial export surplus. It was when that surplus declined during the late 'fifties and during the 'sixties that

Government expenditure abroad came to weaken the dollar.

In the case of Britain the deferred effect of war-time Government spending abroad became a perennial burden on sterling after the war. Military expenditure in India, Egypt and other countries caused an accumulation of large sterling balances by these countries, so that when they spent their sterling after the war the result was large unrequited exports, reducing to that extent Britain's ability to earn foreign exchange through her current exports. This meant that Britain had a correspondingly smaller genuine surplus or a correspondingly larger deficit, leading to the acquisition of sterling balances by other holders even in excess of the amounts accumulated during the war.

Expenditure involved in the British Army of the Rhine and on the East of Suez policy was a perennial drain on sterling. In addition, Britain granted foreign aid which she could ill afford. Although small compared with American foreign aid, for a long time the latter was financed largely out of genuine surpluses, while Britain had seldom adequate surpluses out of which she could have afforded to be generous. Of course there is another side to it — had it not been for our presence East of Suez, the confiscation of British assets would have deprived the U.K. of their yield.

The outstanding example of foreign exchange crises through Government spending abroad was the collapse of the mark after the first World War. Although it had many other causes, the financing of reparations out of non-existent surpluses had powerfully contributed to it. To a high degree the deficit was met through exporting mark notes which had a large market abroad. Even if the Government itself did not raise foreign exchange through exporting notes, which was done entirely on private initiative, the depreciation of the mark abroad far in excess of the fall in its domestic purchasing power was largely the result of external payments of reparations out of non-existent surpluses.

If a country pursues an ambitious military or political policy involving large spendings abroad, or if it is magnanimous in supporting foreign countries with gifts and official loans, it is liable to have to face foreign exchange crises unless Government spending abroad is within the limits of genuinely earned surpluses. To that end domestic consumption would have to be kept down to the extent that is necessary in order to earn such surpluses. Otherwise it means overspending abroad which has the same effect as a trade deficit. Excessive premature military spending or economic or military aid abroad reduces the country's future capacity to help foreign countries later when the granting of such help becomes a vital necessity for the purpose of its foreign policy.

Even external Government payments made out of surpluses undermine the exchange in the long run and prepare the ground for future crises if they prevent the country from accumulating an adequate reserve for future contingencies. They use up the surpluses and prevent the country from making provisions during its seven fat years to meet its needs during its seven lean years.

In any case it is a poor argument to try to excuse foreign exchange difficulties on the ground that they are 'merely' due to Government spending abroad and not to a trade deficit and argue that the economy is basically sound. After all, a Government should be in a better position to keep its own spending under strict control than to influence the choice between goods produced in various countries by many hundreds of millions of people belonging to a hundred nations.

The spending of non-existent surpluses carries dangerous possibilities even for a country which can afford to spend out of reserve. Thus the U.S. sacrificed in ten years her erstwhile impregnable international financial power by halving the gold reserve, at the same time as greatly increasing her short-term indebtedness to foreign holders of dollars.

As for Britain, even though some of the post-war years produced balance of payments surpluses, excessive external Government payments prevented the accumulation of a reserve that would have enabled her to face the subsequent years of large import surpluses with comparative equanimity. But then it is a British tradition to maintain the stability of sterling on a shoestring. The British gold reserve has always been relatively small, and any increase over the indispensable minimum encourages the pursuit of policies that lead to a decline of the reserve. It discourages prudent policies that would maintain and further increase the reserve.

The tradition of managing with a small reserve was the result of Britain's impregnable position during the 19th century when there were perennial export surpluses and large and increasing amounts of foreign investments. In any case, since Britain held large liquid short-term claims against foreign countries, a high Bank rate was at any time able, in the words of Bagehot, to draw money even from the moon. In present changed circumstances a high Bank rate was unable during the crises of 1964–69 to draw enough funds even from places much more accessible than the moon. The same arguments which justified running the gold standard with a bare minimum of gold reserve no longer justify spending the reserve on external Government payments when there are no current surpluses available for it.

External Government spending by the U.S. and the U.K. has greatly increased the risk of foreign exchange crises. Has it been worth while to run the risk for the sake of the advantages derived from that expenditure? The U.S. was until recently under an illusion that economic or military aid bought her friends. They have yet to learn what the U.K. has known for a long time — that biting the hand that feeds them, before, during and after feeding, has become a favourite international sport in some countries receiving foreign aid. As for military bases and armies abroad, their high cost in terms of pressure on the exchanges means premature waste of financial ammunition before the enemy is within range. The maintenance of large gold reserves that would be available might be a better method of securing allies when they are really needed. The possession of a strong and well-secured currency is a better basis for making and retaining friends than the hope that recipients of aid which the donor can ill afford would be duly grateful. It is not past record for generosity but future capacity to be generous that really matters. It would be more statesmanlike to confine foreign aid at the present stage to a few select countries of first-rate importance in terms of world strategy, rather than fritter it away among friend and foe.

Foreign exchange requirements arising from Government spending abroad are not covered as a rule in the market, unless the Central Bank acting for the Government concerned does not possess the particular exchanges required. Even then the operation is usually arranged in such a way as to minimise its effect on exchange rates. Nevertheless, such operations reduce the reserves and increase official foreign liabilities. As a result they tend to weaken the resistance of the exchange to market pressure due to other causes, thereby contributing towards the creation of conditions in which foreign exchange crises are liable to occur.

CHAPTER FIVE

OVEREXPORTING CAPITAL

In an ideal world all surplus countries would export long-term capital to the amount of their current balance of payments surpluses, deficit countries would import a corresponding amount of long-term capital, and everybody would live happily — at any rate as far as foreign exchange is concerned. In a real world discrepancies between current balances and off-setting long-term capital movements are the rule and the absence of discrepancies an exception. Very often surplus countries export less long-term capital than their surpluses, and consequently there is a buying pressure on their exchanges and a selling pressure on the exchanges of deficit countries unable to import long-term capital to cover the amount of their current deficits.

An uneasy equilibrium is liable to become established through short-term debts and claims balancing the discrepancies. So long as the amounts to be covered by these short-term debts and claims are not excessive and the debtor's currency is trusted they need not give cause to crisis. But frequently they are excessive, and the process in which such foreign short-term borrowing is brought about is itself apt to be greatly disturbing to the stability of exchanges. It is very often because deficit countries are unable to import sufficient long-term capital that their exchanges undergo a balance of payments crisis resulting in a depreciation or a rise in interest rates which attracts more capital, or occasioning official intervention which entails official short-term borrowing abroad unless there is enough reserve to support the exchange.

Another source of potential trouble to exchange stability is if countries export long-term capital in excess of their current surplus, or indeed in the complete absence of any exportable surplus. It has the same effect as excessive Government spending abroad, with the difference that the resulting trans-actions are not settled between Central Banks but go through the market mechanism. Overexporting of capital gives rise to selling pressure on the exchange. It tends to deplete the reserves, thereby rendering the exchange more vulnerable when selling pressure arises through other causes. Usually the net result is either a decline of the reserve or re-borrowing on short-term what is lent on long-term, or, as in the case of the U.S., a combination of both.

Britain has been overexporting capital on a large scale during the 'fifties and 'sixties. Her official spokesmen proudly claim credit for the increase of her foreign portfolio investments and direct investments, without admitting that, taking the country as a unit, such investments have been acquired with the aid of borrowed money to the extent to which they have exceeded export surpluses. It is the result of official policy, or in a negative sense, at any rate, of the absence of policy, not to limit capital exports to genuine surpluses, even though it is inevitable that the difference must be financed through an increase in Britain's indebtedness to foreign countries, and that sterling tends to depreciate in the process. What usually happens is that the resulting official support leads to official short-term borrowing abroad.

This attitude is in keeping with British tradition built up during the 19th century when there was no danger in over-lending. It is a familiar free-trader assumption that any pur-chasing power created abroad, whether through buying more foreign goods and services or through lending or investing more money abroad, is bound to come back sooner or later to Britain. Even if it is spent immediately in third countries it would go round and round from country to country until it finds its way back to Britain in the form of increased British visible or invisible exports. This is why the idea of tied loans whose proceeds must be spent in the lending country was strange to 19th-century Britons and remained for a long time unpopu-lar with 20th-century Britons.

The free-trader theory worked in practice only so long as Britain held most of the trumps. She had had the advantage of being first in the field of industrialisation, occupying for a long time a quasi-monopolistic position in respect of textiles, engineering and other goods, and of being able to quote lower prices than her foreign rivals in respect of a further range of goods. It appeared reasonable to assume that any spending or lending abroad would result in sooner or later, directly or indirectly, an increase of buying British goods. In any event temporary discrepancies did not matter because a high Bank rate was able to make good any deficiency in the demand for sterling.

Today the situation is different. Britain is no longer in a position to afford to lend abroad in the form of long-term loans or in the form of direct investments on the assumption that the proceeds of her capital exports would be spent in Britain. Her lending now assumes mainly the form of direct investments. Such investments usually increase current exports of capital goods. But such exports do not benefit the immediate foreign exchange position because they are not paid for. In industries which work to capacity this means a net loss of immediately paying exports.

Nor is this all. The British-owned branch factory abroad increases the total sales of the firm abroad, but it may mean that less will be exported by the U.K. parent factory or other U.K. firms. In any case, most of the proceeds of the affiliate's sales remain abroad, having been paid out in wages and other costs. Only part of the net profits is repatriated in the form of dividends or possibly transfers of undistributed profits.

If the affiliate is sold or is closed down the proceeds of its realised assets may be repatriated; otherwise it takes many years before the repatriated dividends would make up for the exchange loss resulting from the capital export. This is even more the case if instead of constructing a plant with the aid of machinery exported from the U.K. a factory is constructed with local equipment, or if an existing factory is bought with the aid of capital transferred from the U.K. for that purpose.

To some extent such transactions can be financed locally, but the British authorities have been very liberal even during years of sterling crises in granting permits to transfers for that purpose, although in many instances the transfers had to be made through the acquisition of investment dollars representing the proceeds of realised British investments abroad.

If the transfer has to go through the ordinary market, or if it leads to an immediate decline of paying exports, the resulting pressure on sterling may become a contributory cause to an acute crisis. Or it may weaken sterling's resistance to chronic or acute selling pressure. The question is, is it worth while to run that risk for the sake of the advantages secured by the export of capital? The answer varies according to the nature of the investment. If it is for setting up a sales or servicing organisation assisting in the export of U.K. products, then the answer might be in the affirmative. But if it is to set up a branch factory or to buy a rival factory, then it is very much open to question whether the result justifies the loss of reserves. Much depends also how soon and to what extent the investment is likely to become profitable and what chances are for its capital appreciation.

A transaction involving capital export that is distinctly advantageous for the firm concerned is not necessarily advantageous for the country as an economic unit. It is certainly not the case if factories in the U.K. do not work to capacity, or if by setting up factories abroad they are likely to cease to work to capacity. Orders are liable to be transferred to the affiliate, because their cost of production is lower or their delivery dates shorter and more dependable. It might be profitable for the firm to do so, but it entails losses of exports for the country.

The effect of export of capital through direct investment on the exchanges or on exporting capacity may be offset by the import of foreign capital through direct investment. Such reciprocal investment has in fact been proceeding on a large scale during the last decade or more, especially between the U.S. and the U.K. Those arguing in favour of free export and unhampered overexport of capital do so in part on the basis of the advantages they hope to derive from this growing internationalisation — division of labour, acquisition of each other's knowhow, etc. What they overlook is that if they claim that British overseas investments are a second line of defence for sterling, they have to admit that foreign investments in Britain correspondingly weaken that defence. They cannot have it both ways. Foreign holders of investments in the U.K. are in a position to realise their investments and withdraw the proceeds. They are also in a position to hedge against their sterling investments, which is not permitted to U.K. investors abroad.

Indeed the disadvantages of reciprocal investment in each other's countries go far beyond reducing the strength of the second line of defence by the amount of foreign investment in the U.K. Such foreign investment exposes sterling to unilateral pressure through withdrawals of foreign capital or through hedging against it. When sterling is under pressure British investors abroad are not likely to realise their holdings unless they are compelled to do so by their Government, because they do not want to forgo their chances of benefiting by a devaluation of sterling. So pressure due to withdrawals or hedging by foreign holders of sterling assets is not offset by corresponding operations on British investors' account.

In actual practice 'reciprocal' investment is liable to create unilateral pressure on sterling.

Checking or reversing the trend of foreign investment is liable to cause embarrassment to the receiving country, as European countries had good reason to discover for themselves in 1965–66 when U.S. authorities called a halt to American investment abroad and pressed the parent firms to finance their affiliates by raising capital and credits abroad.

The experience of the U.S. during the late 'fifties and the 'sixties confirms the contention that increased investment abroad may become in a given circumstance a source of weakness rather than a source of strength. Since the war the U.S. plunged enthusiastically into the policy of encouraging direct investment in Europe. To a large extent the acquisitions led to a fall in the gold reserve, and were therefore responsible for the series of dollar scares throughout the period. To an even larger extent they led to an increase of foreign short-term balances in the U.S. Their size makes the dollar much more vulnerable.

Nor is it advisable to ignore the political aspects of this policy of deliberate over-investment. Nowadays countries investing abroad may be said to give hostages to fortune. They expose their capital to hostile legislation and taxation, and to nationalisation without adequate compensation, and in many countries they expose their staffs to the xenophobia of the local peoples. The more foreign capital is invested in a country the stronger becomes the temptation of achieving popularity through a confiscation of foreign property, which means a Leftward swing of the domestic and foreign policies of the countries concerned.

This argument applies not only to the developing countries but also to advanced countries such as Italy or France which have large Communist parties. But even if we disregarded such a risk, we should not forget the effect of the financing of investment of American capital in Europe by European dollar balances on General de Gaulle's attitude. While his hostility to the U.S. and to Britain dated back to the war, it had undoubtedly increased by the evidence of U.S. firms buying up French and other continental firms with the aid of capital borrowed from Europe. But for the willingness of the continental countries and others to hold dollar balances the overexporting of American capital would have resulted long ago in a decline of the American gold reserve below danger level. It was largely for this reason that General de Gaulle had been pursuing a crusade against the gold exchange standard which made this system possible. His policy had inflicted on the U.S. a considerable loss of gold, through withdrawals by France and by other countries following her example. To that extent it had weakened the defences of the dollar and had increased the risk of dollar crises.

The direct and indirect effect of overexporting capital in

excess of genuine surpluses has led to the actual or potential weakening of sterling and the dollar and has therefore increased considerably the risk of an international foreign exchange crisis. Any wholesale repatriation of the short-term balances created through over-investment, in addition to hedging against longer investments, is liable to create major pressure on the foreign exchanges of the loaning countries.

It must be borne in mind that the financing of foreign long-term investment by means of short-term borrowing abroad — whether in the form of attracting foreign balances or of borrowing Euro-currencies — is contrary to the elementary principles of sound banking and finance.

Of course it is easy to produce figures to show that in the long run countries which were not afraid of overexporting capital during the 'fifties and 'sixties have recovered most of their investments in dividends and capital gains. But in the short run overexporting capital necessarily means additional pressure on the exchange calling for deflationary measures which result in loss of production. That item must surely be taken into account when forming an opinion whether a country can afford to disregard its immediate foreign exchange problems for the sake of benefits to accrue from its excessive investment in the more distant future.

This does not mean that we must necessarily conform to the over-quoted Keynesian remark that 'in the long run we are all dead'. I am sure Keynes only intended it as a wisecrack and not as a philosophical principle that only short-run considerations matter. We all have to strike compromises between our conflicting long-run and short-run interests. On the whole it is a sound rule that countries should only export their genuinely earned surpluses instead of exposing themselves to foreign exchange crises by exporting non-existent surpluses. But temporary departures from that rule, within reason, can do little harm.

Throughout this chapter we were concerned with overexporting long-term capital. Overlending abroad can assume, however, also the form of excessive short-term credits. That practice is not as dangerous as excessive export of capital in the form of direct investments or long-term loans abroad, or the purchase of foreign long-term securities. In normal conditions creditors should be in a position to call in their short-term credits when the money is required to meet heavy withdrawals of foreign balances or pressure on the exchange due to other causes. But in abnormal conditions short-term credits are liable to become frozen. This is what happened in 1931 when Britain was unable to meet the run on the pound by obtaining a repayment of her short-term credits abroad, owing to the moratorium in Central Europe and elsewhere.

It would be a mistake to assume that the alternative to overexporting capital would necessarily be a corresponding increase of the reserve. Given the traditional British policy of abstaining from accumulating reserves much beyond the indispensable minimum, it seems probable that the alternative to spending on overexporting capital would be spending on increasing current imports. Large reserves would encourage policies which produce that result. From the point of view of sterling's strength overexporting of capital is a smaller evil than overimporting goods.

CHAPTER SIX

WITHDRAWALS OF
FOREIGN BALANCES

For the purposes of this book the term 'foreign balances' is employed in a broad sense. It includes not only balances on current accounts but also bank deposits, funds invested in the money market and in the Euro-currency markets, holdings of Treasury bills and other bills, and even funds invested in short-dated Government or other easily marketable securities. There is no rigid borderline between such 'balances' and foreign holdings of long-term securities or equities which can easily be realised and converted into liquid balances, unless this is prevented by exchange control, as it was in Britain. Foreign balances may be owned by foreign banks on their own account, or they may hold them on account of their non-resident customers, or foreign customers may have accounts of their own with banks in the country whose currency they hold.

There is a wide variety of reasons for which foreign balances are liable to be withdrawn on a sufficiently large scale to affect the foreign exchange position materially. The following are the most important among them:

(1) Fears of devaluation or depreciation.
(2) Fears of exchange control.
(3) Fears of bank failures.
(4) Fears of hostile legislation or prohibitive taxation.
(5) Political instability, or fears of political instability.
(6) War or fears of war.
(7) More lucrative employment possibilities abroad.
(8) Increase of confidence in the holder's own currency or in some other currency.
(9) Holders may require the money for their own use.

(10) Holders may be compelled by their Government to repatriate.

As far as withdrawals for fear of devaluation or depreciation are concerned, the alternative solution is covering hitherto uncovered balances by means of forward exchange transactions, provided that this can be done at a sufficiently low cost to make it worth while. It has to be done sometimes regardless of cost, because banks and merchants may have to keep the money in foreign currencies. They may reduce their balances to a minimum and cover what they are unable to withdraw. To the extent to which balances are covered the direct pressure is on the forward rate. Likewise, if holders of balances are unable or unwilling to effect the transfer until a later date they may sell forward their holdings of foreign currency. In all other instances the pressure is on the spot exchange.

Withdrawals of foreign balances usually play an important part in foreign exchange crises, sometimes a decisive part as they did in the sterling crisis of 1931. Their relative importance has increased compared with the inter-war period, because their amounts have increased very considerably. But already between the wars restless movements of foreign balances — popularly known as 'hot money' — from one centre to another, seeking security from prospective devaluations or depreciations, or trying to benefit from prospective revaluations or appreciations, were often the cause of foreign exchange crises.

Because selling pressure on exchanges is associated with withdrawals of foreign balances both as cause and as effect, those making such withdrawals are often subject to criticism and abuse. The 'gnomes of Zurich' have become a byword in the popular Press, in political debates, and even in serious economic controversies. They are often accused of trying to wreck sterling or any other currency under pressure, by their untimely withdrawals of their balances. While criticism may be justified if the pressure is due to purely speculative selling, it is utterly unjustified to blame any holder of a foreign currency who wants to safeguard his interests by withdrawing his balances under the threat — real or imaginary — of losses through

a devaluation or depreciation. Those who attack them overlook the fact that when the 'gnomes' transferred their funds to
the country concerned they supported its currency to the same
extent to which they are now weakening it. As a net result
their operations are supposed to leave the reserve position of
the country unchanged.

In practice what often happens is that the receiving country
fails to preserve in a liquid form the gain in the reserves obtained
through an influx of foreign funds, so that when those funds are
withdrawn it can ill afford to lose the reserves it has to lose in
order to safeguard the stability of its currency in face of the
resulting pressure. The authorities of such a country have
only themselves to blame for the resulting crisis instead of
blaming the 'gnomes' whom they did not praise for strengthening the currency when the funds were received from them.

Of course it is difficult to expect a country to retain in gold
or foreign exchange the full 100 per cent equivalent of the
foreign funds transferred there. There is bound to be strong
inducement to take things easy thanks to the growth of the
reserves. The receiving country is tempted to pursue more
expansionary domestic policies and to abstain from resisting
the resulting upward trend of prices and other inflationary
symptoms. In face of the rising reserves such resistance would
be politically unpopular. So the effect of overexpansion on
the trade balance is disregarded. There is also temptation to
export capital and to grant credits abroad more freely and to
relax any remaining exchange control measures, to increase
tourist allowances, to adopt a more liberal attitude towards
transferring legacies abroad, etc.

As a result, when the tide turns and the foreign balances are
withdrawn a large part of the surplus reserves is no longer
available to meet the resulting selling pressure on sterling. To
prevent a depreciation the country concerned has then to run
down its reserve towards danger level and has to raise foreign
credits in a haste. It also has to adopt unpopular measures to
reinforce the domestic economy. It is because of the unpopularity of such measures that the 'gnomes' are blamed. What

is forgotten is that when the flow of foreign funds was inward it enabled the authorities to keep credit cheaper and more plentiful than they could have done in the absence of this movement of funds. This attitude confirms the saying that one makes an enemy by lending.

This subject has been discussed at considerable length during the 'sixties in connection with the controversy over London's role as an international banking centre. It was not only the 'gnomes' who were blamed for the series of sterling crises to which withdrawals of foreign balances admittedly contributed, but also the London banks for attracting foreign balances. They were held responsible for the policy of 'stop-go' under which the Government had to introduce restrictive economic measures from time to time in order to safeguard the stability of sterling against the effects of withdrawals of foreign balances. Not only politicians and journalists but even some economists who ought to know better failed to realise that foreign balances have first to come to London in order to be withdrawn. They failed to realise that but for the willingness of foreigners to acquire and hold sterling there would have had to be much more 'stop' and much less 'go' in earlier periods.

Take for instance the enormous sterling balances inherited from the war by India and other countries. They used them up to finance their own deficits. To the extent to which the sterling was spent in the U.K. it meant unrequited exports for which the U.K. received no fresh foreign exchange. But for the willingness of other countries to acquire and hold sterling, the U.K. authorities would have had to deflate ruthlessly in order to fill the hole in the balance of payments created by these unrequited exports. Such facts are of course forgotten — if they had ever been realised — when the withdrawal of these funds threatens to cause a sterling crisis.

The only ground for criticism of the system under which London attracts and retains foreign balances is that the support the influx of such balances gives to sterling is liable to convey a false feeling of security and leads therefore to unwarranted optimistic policies. But that is not the ground on which the system is criticised. If the 'gnomes' were willing to retain their balances in perpetuity their very existence would be ignored. But it is their duty to their customers and to themselves to withdraw the balances whenever they feel that sterling is devaluation prone, or even whenever they can be employed more profitably elsewhere. It is unfair to present them as the villains of the piece, least of all by those who are really responsible for pursuing policies that inspire distrust in sterling.

This diversion was necessary in order to provide a background against which withdrawals on exchanges have to be judged. While there may be some logic in preventing the influx of foreign funds — this has been done by Germany, Switzerland and other countries during the late 'fifties and the 'sixties — it is utterly illogical to receive them with open arms and blame their owners when the balances are withdrawn, and when their withdrawal causes a foreign exchange crisis.

There is a limit — albeit an elastic one — beyond which foreign balances of a certain kind cannot be reduced because their owners need them in the centres concerned. Oft-repeated statements that as a result of recent heavy withdrawals the remaining balances are now at their irreducible minimum level and cannot be reduced further may be listed among 'famous last words'. Anybody relying on this and taking it for granted that there would be no further substantial withdrawals is liable to get unpleasant surprises. Next time the statistics are published he may find that the reductions had been relatively moderate, so that the amounts still held here and liable to withdrawals are still considerable. What often happens is that the balances are not withdrawn in the true sense but merely change hands as between foreign owners. This process may involve transfers from one bank to another, or transfers from bank deposits into loans to Local Authorities. But it does not reduce the total power of foreign holders to realise more sterling.

We saw above that holders of foreign balances are the most-accused villains of the piece — at any rate when they are engaged in withdrawing their holdings. The blame is extended to those banks who hold their accounts. Hence the agitation that London should divest itself from its role of international banker. When such demand came from General de Gaulle, who was anxious that the franc should take sterling's place as an international currency, it was understandable. But on the British side it is based on the wishful thinking that some Santa Claus might relieve Britain of the huge liability represented by foreign balances held in London, in which case it would no longer be necessary to call 'stop' from time to time in order to prevent an efflux. But in such a situation any temporary import surplus would mean borrowing from the international authorities and they might make it conditional upon deflation. The willingness of 'gnomes' and their clients to acquire and hold sterling balances tends to obviate the necessity for the British authorities to go to foreign Central Banks and Treasuries 'cap in hand' in quest of financial assistance. Once London no longer attracts voluntary deposits that humiliating experience would have to occur even more frequently.

CHAPTER SEVEN

FLIGHT OF DOMESTIC CAPITAL

THE absolute and relative importance of the flight of domestic capital among the causes responsible for foreign exchange crises varies considerably according to country, also according to period. It depends largely on the character of the people concerned — whether they are law-abiding and patriotic or otherwise. It also depends on the country's past experience in advanced inflation and exchange depreciation, which largely determines the degree to which the nations have acquired a tradition for getting out of the national currency. The popularity of the Government in office influences the attitude of citizens towards flight of capital. The degree and efficiency of exchange control, the deterrent effect of penalties for evasion, and the extent of temptation to evade it, have all a share in determining the extent to which flight of domestic capital causes or aggravates foreign exchange crises.

The causes for a flight of national capital are more or less the same as those enumerated and examined in the last chapter with reference to withdrawals of foreign money. Their relative importance, is, however, not the same. With the exception of countries which had had recent experience in advanced currency depreciation, devaluation fears do not play nearly as important a part in inducing flights of domestic capital as in inducing withdrawals of foreign balances. In Britain, for instance, the conception that 'the pound is a pound' was deeply engrained in the public in 1931 and throughout the fluctuations of sterling during the 'thirties, so that there was no indication of any large-scale flight of British capital during that period.

In most countries only the financially sophisticated fringe is liable to engage actively in transferring capital abroad for fear of devaluation — bankers, businessmen, large investors. Even so the total they are in a position to move abroad is probably well in excess of the total of foreign balances liable to be withdrawn. Widespread flight of capital owned by such domestic holders is capable of producing a landslide, especially as it is usually accompanied by pressure through other causes. It is all the more dangerous because, while the authorities may have some idea about the approximate maximum of potential withdrawals of foreign funds, it is difficult to have even a vague idea of the possible limit of potential withdrawals of domestic capital. Repeated devaluations or persistent depreciation might well spread the practice over wider classes with ever-increasing totals involved. In some countries such as France transfers of capital abroad whenever there is trouble assume a nation-wide character.

Fear of exchange control is a distinctly less important cause for the flight of domestic capital than for withdrawals of foreign balances. But it cannot be ignored. Importers may wish to build up reserves abroad in order to be able to secure the continuity of essential supplies. Other residents may be tempted to accumulate a nest-egg abroad. The sophisticated fringe which is liable to transfer capital abroad for fear of devaluation is inclined to act even in the absence of acute fear — to ensure that if and when the risk should become acute they should not be precluded from taking precautions. Differences in yield are only liable to affect decisions by banks and large firms or investors whether to transfer funds abroad.

While distrust in all local banks of a country might give rise to a flight of domestic capital abroad, it is more likely to lead to note hoarding, gold hoarding and the accumulation of other tangible assets. For one thing, depositors in the leading countries realise that a general bank crisis in their country would not remain confined to their country but would have grave international repercussions, so that they would not seek safety in transferring their capital into foreign currencies or to foreign banks.

Fears of hostile class-war legislation, prohibitive taxation, political instability or war are likely to cause a flight of domestic capital on an extensive scale in countries whose peoples are in the habit of thinking in terms of capital flight. In Latin America, for instance, such influences are liable to assume first-rate importance. Even in more settled countries threats of war or civil war are liable to cause exchanges to depreciate, and it is through fears of such depreciation rather than of war or civil war that domestic capital is liable to find its way abroad in large amounts. We must also remember that in all Western countries there are now many thousands of former refugees who have settled down and have acquired fortunes in their adopted countries, but who still remember their inter-war insecurity. At the first indication of trouble they are inclined instinctively to play for safety. In most countries it is such capital that is likely to aggravate foreign exchange crises, long before old residents begin to think of playing for safety.

Even in the absence of exchange control affecting residents, various official and unofficial measures tend to discourage the outflow of domestic capital. In the U.S. the unofficial ban on such operations that has been in force since 1965 is now official. The rule under which American banks are under obligation to report to the fiscal authorities the withdrawal of large amounts of notes also tends to increase the difficulties of an outflow of capital which assumes largely the form of exporting notes across the Canadian frontier.

Such exports of notes have long been a favourite method of flight of capital. It assumed gigantic proportion in Germany after the first World War. During the inter-war period it was one of the methods by which large French funds found their way to Switzerland. That country has long been the haven for flight capital and Basle is still the principal market in foreign notes. The flight from the lira in the 'sixties assumed the form of smuggling notes into Switzerland. There are many other more refined methods, but their description on these pages would not be in the public interest. Even the U.K. is far from immune from flight of capital through the smuggling of notes. The U.K. is also exposed to unauthorised capital outflow through the operation of the Sterling Area system which covers a multitude of leaks. In the 'fifties the 'Kuwait gap' and the 'Hong Kong gap' received wide publicity, but there are many other loopholes.

Yet relatively speaking there has not been much flight of British domestic capital. As already observed, there was virtually none during the crisis of 1931 or during the ups and downs of sterling in the following years. Nor was there much flight of American capital from the U.S. in the 'thirties, presumably because conditions appeared to be equally insecure in every country and in every currency. During the second World War, under war-time control and amidst war-time patriotic atmosphere, flight of domestic capital became difficult if not impossible. After the war, however, exchange control became gradually relaxed and patriotism gave way to resentment over policies of improvident Governments, some of them more or less hostile to business interests and to investors. There was once more much flight of capital from France, also from other countries. In addition to Switzerland, certain centres assumed importance as havens for refugee capital. They included Tangier, Liechtenstein, Luxembourg and some South American centres.

Except when the flight of capital assumes the form of the smuggling out of hoarded gold, precious stones, objects of art, etc., it increases pressure on the national exchange of the loaning country. When it assumes the form of the export of notes, the notes are sold abroad and are repatriated by the banks who acquire them. They are in a position to sell the proceeds, thereby aggravating the selling pressure. Even if there is a ban on re-importing the notes they somehow find their way back gradually if their depreciation to a discount makes it profitable to smuggle them back.

In Britain and in other countries a system is in operation under which domestic buyers of foreign securities can only pay with the proceeds of foreign securities sold by other domestic holders, so that an outflow of capital through that channel is thereby avoided. But if the premium on such special investment currencies rises to a high level there is a strong temptation to circumvent this system.

To a large degree refugee capital constitutes a hidden asset for the country, and it might become a source of strength in the future. Thus France gained considerable financial power twice within the last 40 years, in 1926–28 and again in the sixties, when French residents repatriated the large amounts they had accumulated abroad during periods of uncertainty. Unfortunately such hidden reserves are inclined to remain hidden when their repatriation would be a godsend to the exchange under pressure. They are only likely to be repatriated when the tide has definitely turned so that the exchange could hold its own even without such repatriations. Moreover much of the capital is liable to remain abroad permanently, in particular if their owners emigrate and settle abroad. Under British exchange control regulations emigrants are entitled to remit up to £5,000 of their capital, also any legacies they inherit after their emigration. The over-generous travel allowance of £250 per journey, too, provided opportunities before 1966 for the accumulation of capital abroad.

Apart from tightening exchange control and stiffening penalties, an effective method of discouraging flight of capital is a credit squeeze at home. Firms who find it difficult to finance their businesses might feel compelled to abstain from sending more money abroad, and even to repatriate some of their capital as an alternative to having to curtail their business activities at home for lack of credit facilities. Such situations are liable to arise during prolonged periods of foreign exchange crises. In any case an effective credit squeeze is apt to inspire confidence in the currency and is apt to improve the basic strength of the currency, so that it tends to reinforce the exchange apart altogether from enforcing repatriations of flight moneys.

CHAPTER EIGHT

PURE SPECULATION

WE saw in earlier chapters that there are various ways in which it is possible to speculate — in the broadest sense of the term — on the devaluation of a currency. Merchants and industrialists may increase their stocks of imported goods beyond their normal requirements. They may delay export of goods whose prices are fixed in foreign currencies. They may cover well in advance the foreign currencies required for their imports, and they may delay the sale of the foreign exchange proceeds of their exports invoiced in foreign currencies by granting longer credits to their customers abroad. Non-resident holders of assets in the devaluation-prone currency may hedge for amounts in excess of the actual risk involved, or they may undo their hedges and restore them again and again, according to the view they take about devaluation prospects. These methods of speculation will be dealt with in greater detail in subsequent chapters. In the present chapter we are concerned with speculation in the narrower and more popular use of the term — the creation and maintenance of short positions in foreign exchanges solely for the purpose of being able to earn a capital profit if the currencies concerned should be devalued or if they should depreciate.

Speculation in exchanges can assume the form of bull speculation as well as bear speculation. But buying pressure on an exchange, inconvenient as it may be to the country concerned in given circumstances, is not a foreign exchange crisis. It only comes within the scope of this book in so far as such buying pressure tends to be to the detriment of the foreign exchange position of countries whose currencies are sold against the revaluation-prone currency. In 1969, for instance, revaluation-prone D. marks were bought against evaluation-prone sterling and French francs, with the result that selling pressure against sterling and the franc was probably even heavier than it would have been if speculators had not anticipated a revaluation of the D. mark at the same time as anticipating a devaluation of sterling and the franc. In 1961 both sterling and dollars were sold against D. marks, Swiss francs and Dutch guilders mainly because a revaluation of these currencies was anticipated. This bull speculation aggravated the problem of defending sterling and even that of defending the dollar.

Pure speculation assumes the form of selling for forward delivery currencies that the seller does not possess and does not expect to possess. Or it may assume the form of borrowing devaluation-prone currencies and selling the spot exchange, in the hope that by the time the loan falls due it would be possible to cover its amount at a more favourable exchange rate. It may also assume the form of selling of the national currency by residents, even though that practice is handicapped by exchange control in most countries, or by non-resident holders who would have to replenish their holdings sooner or later.

The development of an active market in forward exchanges after the first World War greatly increased the possibilities of pure speculation. So long as speculation was confined to the sale of spot exchanges it was necessarily limited by the amount of spot exchanges available to speculators for selling or obtainable by them through borrowing. It is true, residents of the country concerned were in a position to sell large amounts of their national currency. But non-residents' holdings of the currency were necessarily limited and so was their capacity to borrow in that currency. Supplies of spot exchanges could be curtailed drastically by official monetary policy through creating tight money conditions and through raising interest rates so as to raise the cost of speculation with the aid of borrowed money.

On the other hand, in order to operate in the forward exchange market, speculators need not possess the currencies they sell. It is true, banks in the 'twenties required sellers of forward currencies to deposit a certain percentage of the amount sold, so as to be safeguarded against losses in case the rates should go against speculators who might not be able to meet their commitments under the contract. But well-known customers were not subjected to that practice. Nor is it applied to dealings between banks. Banks themselves, in their dealings with each other, fix a maximum limit to outstanding forward commitments in relation to every other bank. Even so, the grand totals of those limits are usually very large and they are apt to be elastic, so that the total capacity of all speculators to go short by selling an exchange forward is indeed very extensive.

In the late 'fifties the potentialities of speculating by means of selling borrowed spot exchanges have also increased considerably as a result of the development and expansion of the Euro-currency markets. It has greatly facilitated borrowing for speculative purposes. Until its advent speculators wanting to sell spot exchange had to borrow the currency concerned in its own country. Now they can borrow it in the Euro-currency markets. Since 1969 they can do so on a vast scale.

This means that, while prior to the existence of those markets the monetary authorities of the countries whose currencies came under pressure were in a position to restrict the amounts of their currencies available for speculators to borrow and sell, now they are to a large degree helpless, because they have no control over the amounts of Euro-currencies available for that purpose or over the rates at which they are available. In particular for the requirements of speculation in anticipation of a devaluation over the week-end there are large amounts of Euro-currencies available, even if the rates for such short deposits in devaluation-prone Euro-sterling or other Euro-currencies are apt to rise to very high level whenever there is an acute devaluation scare.

Although, as pointed out above, residents of countries with devaluation-prone currencies are handicapped by exchange control from engaging in speculation through selling short their national currencies, this does not apply to banks. In most countries they are allowed, for the sake of ensuring the smooth working of the foreign exchange market, to have short positions up to an authorised limit. In theory they are not supposed to exceed these limits, but in practice this only means that their short positions must be reduced to the authorised limits for the dates for which they have to make their returns to be submitted to their authorities. But even if they were to submit returns at closing time every day — which rule came to be applied to some U.K. banks in 1969 — it would still be possible to exceed the limits during the course of a business day and cover the excess before closing. Moreover, the official limits refer to net official positions, being the balance between the amounts of long positions in some exchanges and those of short positions in others. This means that there is no legal limit to the amount of forward dollars sold against forward D. marks or *vice versa*.

Admittedly the need for covering for the purposes of the weekly returns does handicap speculation to a large extent, because banks want to avoid having to cover in haste at an unfavourable moment. Nevertheless, even though the importance of speculation by banks should not be overrated, they might initiate in given circumstances movements of exchange rates that could become self-aggravating. Hence the decision of the British authorities in 1966 to reduce the permitted limit of open positions in the case of a number of authorised dealers.

Taking everything into account it seems that speculation is not nearly as harmful to an exchange as an adverse trade balance, or a lengthening of leads and lags, withdrawal of foreign funds, flight of national capital, or even hedging by foreign investors against their direct investment. Sooner or later speculative positions have to be covered, which means that a large short position is a potential source of strength. But if the cause for speculation persists then that potential source of strength is of little immediate use. It certainly failed to help sterling during the acute attacks on it in 1964–69.

Even if it is beyond question that short positions have to be covered sooner or later, selling short is frequently the main cause of acute foreign exchange crises, or it aggravates foreign exchange crises due to other causes, to an extent as to cause permanent damage to the currency, especially under systems of flexible parities or floating exchange rates. The destructive dynamic effects of speculative selling lie largely in their psychological effects. Evidence of speculative pressure is liable to induce foreign holders to withdraw their balances, merchants to lengthen their leads and lags, and foreign investors to hedge. It might even induce flight of national capital. Any devaluation or depreciation caused by speculative pressure is liable to become non-reversible, and if so it causes a permanent fall in the domestic value of the currency concerned.

Official support to the forward exchange that is under speculative attack is justified, always provided that the authorities have good reason for assuming that the attack is purely or mainly speculative. Since the sellers do not possess the sterling they are unable to claim on maturity the delivery of the foreign exchanges sold for forward delivery unless and until they have bought the national currency needed to pay for them. This means that in face of purely speculative pressure the authorities are safe in going short in foreign currencies without running any risk other than the possibility of a financial loss if, contrary to their expectations, they should have to devalue before the forward contracts mature. The adoption of the policy of official support to the forward exchange has therefore gone a long way towards reducing the damaging effects of pure speculation. Unfortunately the use of that device has not been confined to defending the exchanges against speculative attack. From November 1964 until the devaluation of sterling three years later it was used for concealing basic weaknesses.

In practice it is extremely difficult to ascertain the extent to which pressure on an exchange is due to pure speculation. It is too tempting for the authorities to assume or pretend to assume the speculative character of a movement which has other causes, and to defend the exchange by the easy way of supporting the forward exchange, in order to obviate the necessity for borrowing abroad and for adopting unpopular measures to strengthen the currency. To avoid this it is

expedient in doubtful cases to assume the non-speculative
character of the pressure, or to assume that speculative selling
is justified by some basic weakness which calls for basic remedies. This subject is dealt with in greater detail in Chapter 22.

Pure speculation played a decisive part on many occasions in
the inter-war period. Speculative attacks were responsible for
the series of crises of the German mark, the French and Belgian
francs, the lira and other currencies. In a large number of
instances speculators succeeded in forcing the hands of Governments to devalue their currencies or to allow them to depreciate.
In the summer of 1931 the main pressure on sterling was due
to withdrawals of foreign balances, but speculative selling
powerfully contributed towards forcing the Government to
suspend the gold standard and allow sterling to find its level.
Its ups and downs during the 'thirties, and those of other
currencies, were largely due to speculative activities. They
assumed such extent that they forced the countries of the Gold
Bloc to devalue their currencies in 1936.

During the post-war period, too, speculation played an
important part in the creation and accentuation of currency
scares. It influenced the fluctuations of the franc and the lira
during the 'forties and the 'fifties. It was partly responsible
for the attacks on sterling in 1956, 1957 and 1961, and for the
crisis of 1967 on the eve of the devaluation when the Government ceased to disclaim its intention to devalue.

Although many banks take a hand in pure speculation,
they are now inclined to discourage their clients from doing
so. During the inter-war period, especially in the 'twenties,
there was a great deal of non-banking speculation by professional speculators, and even the general public joined in whenever there was a sweeping speculative movement. Since the
war most banks refuse obviously speculative business. It is no
longer possible for any stranger to open a speculative account
with a bank through depositing a margin to safeguard the
bank against losses.

Most banks only transact forward exchange with non-banking clients with whose business they are familiar, and are only

prepared to undertake transactions for those who have a legitimate interest to cover or to hedge against. This is so especially when there is strong pressure on a currency, and when there is a possibility that the forward markets might become congested because most banks have reached their maximum limits up to which they are prepared to take the names of most other banks. In such situations banks are anxious to reserve their facilities for legitimate clients. There is nowadays enough genuine business to keep them occupied and they do not feel tempted to cater for speculative clients.

Even so, banks are unable to discriminate against speculative operations when dealing with other banks. In the foreign exchange market no questions are ever asked about the purpose or motives of the proposed transactions. While a bank is in a position to refuse suspected speculative buying or selling orders by its non-banking customers — unless of course the account is too important to risk its transfer to some other bank — it is not in a position to know whether the deal offered by another bank is speculative or not. It is reasonable to assume that whenever the market is very active as a result of an acute or impending crisis a relatively high proportion of the turnover is speculative.

Speculative selling usually runs concurrently with increased selling through hedging and through a lengthening of leads and lags. They affect each other reciprocally and it is impossible to tell which is the cause and which is the effect. Speculation, by widening forward margins, tends to increase the volume of outward interest arbitrage, which again, by reducing the reserves, tends further to stimulate speculative selling. This cause of foreign exchange crises is discussed in Chapter 11.

CHAPTER NINE

HEDGING

THE subject of hedging as a cause of foreign exchange crises has already been touched upon briefly in several chapters. In view of its great importance, however, and also owing to the inadequate extent to which its importance is realised even to-day, it is necessary to examine it in much greater detail. Although covering against exchange risk is a familiar practice, much less is known outside the circles directly concerned about hedging against exchange risks. Even economists specialising in forward exchange are inclined to use the two terms indiscriminately as if they were synonymous, without appearing to realise the fundamental practical as well as theoretical difference between covering and hedging.

Covering aims at insuring against devaluation risk on self-liquidating transactions involving a definite amount and having a definite maturity date. Hedging concerns transactions which are not self-liquidating and on which the risk is not of a definite amount, because the realisable value of the assets concerned is uncertain, and because the effect of a devaluation on their value is in any case uncertain. While covering aims at avoiding speculative risks hedging amounts to assuming a speculative risk in order to safeguard oneself against a bigger speculative risk in the opposite sense. Covering closes what would otherwise be an open position, while hedging creates an open position which is only offset very approximately by the value of the assets against which one is hedging.

There are the following main types of hedging transactions:
(1) Hedging against the exchange risk on holdings of foreign securities.
(2) Hedging against the exchange risk on direct investments abroad.

(3) Hedging against the risk of depreciation of inventories of goods whose prices are liable to be affected by a change of parities.

It is a widespread practice to hedge against the devaluation risk on holdings of foreign securities if the currency of the country concerned comes to be regarded as devaluation-prone. Such operations are often linked with speculation on the appreciation of Government loans and other securities that is expected to follow a devaluation owing to the fall in interest rates made possible by the devaluation. Thus during the middle 'thirties large amounts of French *rentes* were held in foreign countries, partly because owing to the measures adopted in defence of the franc the yield was high and partly because there were good prospects of a capital gain through their appreciation after the fall of interest rates following on a devaluation. Holders had to safeguard themselves against a capital loss through the devaluation of the franc. From time to time the discount on forward francs widened and the cost of hedging became prohibitive, so that it induced many holders to close their accounts.

History repeated itself in Britain during the prolonged sterling crisis of 1964–67. Foreign investors bought high-yielding Government loans for the sake of their yield and for the prospects of a capital gain after a devaluation of sterling. Owing to official support of forward sterling that was keeping the forward margin artificially low, the cost of hedging was very low. There was, therefore, much inducement for non-residents to engage in such transactions on a large scale, and there is reason to believe that very considerable amounts were engaged in them. This type of hedging involves swap transactions which support spot sterling and weaken forward sterling.

Much more important than this type of transaction from the point of view of its effect on the forward rate is hedging against direct investments. Its importance has increased considerably during the 'fifties and 'sixties, owing to the expansion in the volume of direct investments. Whenever there was a sterling

C 2

scare American and other firms with subsidiaries or branches in the U.K. hastened to cover by selling forward sterling. Such operations had come to be regarded in the market as an indication of an approaching crisis. Many holders of direct investment were in the habit of undoing their hedges whenever the sterling scare had passed, but owing to the artificially low discount on forward sterling many others deemed it worth their while to maintain their hedges permanently as an insurance against devaluation.

To the extent to which foreign direct investors removed their hedges when sterling was firm and restored them when sterling turned weak they aggravated the selling pressure at a time when sterling was also sold for other causes. The counterpart to the demand for forward dollars was usually supplied by the Bank of England so as to avoid a widening of the discount on forward sterling, even though such a widening might have gone a long way towards discouraging hedging and speculation.

Hedging against direction investments may be a potential source of strength, because foreign firms have to cover sooner or later instead of meeting their forward contracts by selling out their subsidiaries for fear of a devaluation. For this reason the Bank of England need not necessarily lose dollars when its forward contracts arising from such hedging mature. On the other hand, foreign holders of sterling securities acquired for the purpose of benefiting by a capital appreciation that would follow a devaluation would be in a position to pay for the dollars they had bought from the Bank of England, whenever they chose to realise their holdings. To the extent to which such hedging keeps down the decline of the reserve because it causes demand for spot sterling, it represents a potential drain on the reserve instead of an actual drain.

Even official support to meet hedging against direct investment is unable to prevent an increase in the pressure on spot sterling if hedging contracts are not renewed. It is possible and necessary to visualise a number of situations in which hedgers may decide to realise or reduce their assets for reasons other than devaluation fears.

(1) Fears of a tightening of exchange control. Exchange control might prevent direct investors from renewing their hedges, or from renewing them for a conveniently long period. Conceivably it might even stop the fulfilment of existing forward contracts.

(2) The possibility of a change in official forward exchange policy. Unlimited support of the forward rate, which keeps the cost of hedging abnormally low, might be abandoned. Having changed their minds suddenly in 1964 in favour of unlimited intervention which they opposed until then, the U.K. authorities repeated their volte-face in 1967. The mere possibility of such a change is liable to worry foreign holders of direct investments, as they face the risk of the cost of hedging being raised to a prohibitive level.

(3) The possibility of saturation of the forward exchange market. Each bank sets a limit to the total amount for which it is prepared to take the name of every other bank for forward contracts. Saturation point was reached repeatedly during the crises of the 1930s and during 1964–1967 bankers became concerned about that possibility. On the eve of the devaluation some first-class names came to be refused because the limits were reached.

(4) The nationalisation of foreign-owned firms. This is almost certainly followed by repatriation of the amounts received in compensation. Fears of additional nationalisations, combined with suspicions that the Government might not pay fair compensation, are liable to induce foreign firms to dispose of their subsidiaries while the going is good.

(5) Prohibitive taxation and other 'class-war' measures. Under a Labour Government with a substantial majority, which is anxious to appease trade unions and left-wing supporters for wage-restraint, credit squeeze, its Vietnam policy and other matters, such measures are regarded in business quarters as an ever-present possibility.

(6) Intolerable labour troubles. Even if, in themselves, labour difficulties should not be deemed sufficient to induce foreign owners of subsidiaries to withdraw from the U.K., they might decide to shift a high proportion of their orders to their factories outside the U.K., for the sake of shorter and more dependable delivery dates and of lower costs. This would entail the withdrawal of a substantial part of their working capital from the U.K.

(7) Difficulties in the outer Sterling Area. It would require too much space to try even to summarise the wide variety of abnormal risks and difficulties direct investors in the new countries have to face. Recent experience leaves no doubt about the strong possibility that many owners of subsidiaries in the outer Sterling Area might decide to cut their losses and withdraw.

(8) Measures adopted by governments of the investing countries. Faced with grave balance-of-payments problems of their own, they might go so far as to commandeer easily marketable direct investments abroad. Even without going to such lengths, they might force foreign subsidiaries owned by their nationals to repatriate their available reserves. This is what actually happened in 1965 in the U.S. They might also force them to curtail the activities of such subsidiaries, so as to secure immediate relief to the balance of payments from the proceeds of the resulting realisations of raw material stocks and reductions of inventories of manufactures.

These are only some of the most obvious reasons for the repatriation of capital. Several of them are liable to operate simultaneously. While most of them might not suffice in isolation to induce the parent firm to give up its affiliate, the combined influence of several of them might well produce that effect. Allowing for all these possibilities, there seems to be no justification for the optimistic assumption that all, or even most, official forward contracts arising from hedging by direct investors are self-liquidating and that their formidable total need not, therefore, worry the authorities.

Nor is this the whole story by any means. During the life of forward contracts that originate through hedging against direct investments — they are frequently for 12 months — the ownership of the claim for the delivery of dollars against payment of sterling on maturity is liable to change repeatedly. Hedgers may decide, under the influence of more optimistic views about sterling's prospects, to undo the hedge before it matures. This happens, in fact, very frequently. The forward dollars sold by them may find their way, through the intermediary of their banks and of the foreign exchange market, possibly after a series of transactions, into the hands of merchants, financiers, or foreign monetary authorities, who expect to possess the sterling needed to pay for the dollars on maturity, and who intend to use their sterling for that purpose.

Thus the counterpart for the dollars released by former hedgers could be provided as a result of an adverse balance of payments, or of some authorised export of capital, or through withdrawals of funds by a Sterling Area country diversifying its reserve or withdrawing altogether from the Sterling Area. The counterpart could originate from many other sources. What matters from the point of view with which we are here concerned is that, were it not for the undoing of earlier hedges, all these adverse influences would tend to produce immediately their natural adverse effect on sterling and on the reserves. As it is, their effect is neutralised until the forward contracts mature, when the new owners of the claims for dollars can pay for them without first having to buy sterling. As a result the Bank of England loses on maturity the dollars it would have lost earlier in the absence of the sale of dollars by foreign firms undoing their hedges.

Admittedly, losses of reserves would occur in any case through the developments discussed in the last paragraph, as indeed through withdrawals of foreign investments, regardless of whether or not the authorities support the forward rate. The difference is that, as a result of official support, the losses of dollars are deferred and the decline of the reserves is temporarily disguised through assuming the form of unpublished official forward commitments. Such a deferment of the effect of adverse developments suits the authorities who hope that, even in the absence of a basic improvement in the British balance of payments, some miracle in the form of inflation in a major country or crisis in a major currency might reverse the trend, so that even if the Bank of England should be called upon to discharge the forward exchange liabilities eventually, it could do so without losing dollars.

Yet it is in the public interest that adverse trends should be noticed and dealt with as soon as possible and not be allowed to remain concealed. Unlimited support of the forward rate conceals from the public the extent of any fresh weakness. Indeed, even the authorities themselves have no means of knowing what proportion of the ultimate claimants of the dollars they had sold forward are in a position to pay for them in sterling without first having to buy the sterling for that purpose.

The third type of hedging is against the risk on holdings of inventories that are liable to depreciate as a result of a devaluation. The most obvious examples are inventories of goods imported from Britain and the Sterling Area during periods when sterling is under a cloud. A devaluation of sterling would enable importers without stocks to buy British and Sterling Area goods at lower prices, thereby enabling them to undersell their rivals who had acquired such goods before the devaluation. Even if the goods were invoiced in sterling, once they were paid for by their importers they are exposed to losses through a devaluation of sterling so long as they still hold stocks imported before devaluation. To safeguard themselves against it they sell sterling forward to the value of their stocks in hand. An increase of this practice is equivalent to an increase of lags because, although individual British exporters have received the amounts due to them, the country as such does not really benefit by the payment until the short positions created by foreign importers hedging against a devaluation of sterling are closed.

Such hedging operations need not be confined to holdings of British and Sterling Area goods. If as a result of a devaluation of sterling the prices of such goods in terms of the currencies of the importers should decline, it would affect rival goods imported from other countries. To meet the increased competition of cut-price British goods, holders of rival foreign goods — indeed even holders of goods produced in the country of the holders — would have to reduce their prices, too, and might have to sell those goods at a loss. This means that whenever a major currency such as sterling is considered devaluation-prone there is a strong inducement for holders of goods which are liable to be affected by a fall in the prices of the goods imported from the country with the devaluation-prone currency to hedge against possible losses by going short in the devaluation-prone currency.

The extent to which this is actually done depends (a) on the extent to which the currency in question is considered devaluation-prone ; (b) on the extent to which the goods of the country with a devaluation-prone currency are expected to compete with rival goods as a result of a devaluation ; (c) on the cost of the hedging ; and (d) on the extent to which holders of inventories are hedging-minded. Because the cost of hedging against sterling was kept artificially cheap at between $\frac{1}{2}$ per cent and 1 per cent p.a. over a prolonged period, a large number of business firms holding inventories in non-sterling goods got into the habit of hedging by means of selling forward sterling. There is reason to believe that a by no means negligible proportion of the selling pressure on forward sterling came from such transactions. It means that the forward exchange of a major country with a devaluation-prone currency is exposed to very heavy pressure. Indeed, such a country, like Atlas, has to carry the burden of the universe.

All such hedging operations are of course entirely self-liquidating. The hedgers do not possess the sterling they had sold forward, nor are they expected to come into possession of sterling, so that sooner or later they have to close their accounts which will involve the purchase of spot sterling in order to pay for the dollars they had bought. Since the counterpart is represented by a short position in dollars on account of the

Bank of England, the net result leaves sterling and the British reserve unaffected on balance. The hedgers are not likely to close their open positions, however, unless they have regained confidence in sterling, or until they have sold out the inventories hedged against, without replenishing their stocks.

It emerges from the above that hedging in all forms is liable to contribute powerfully towards selling pressure on the currency that is considered devaluation-prone. While hedging against new capital imports provides a welcome if temporary support to the spot exchange concerned, hedging in other forms aggravates the selling pressure on the forward exchange without an offsetting buying pressure on the spot exchange.

Incredible as it may sound, British residents are prevented by exchange control regulations from supporting sterling by hedging against their foreign investments or against their inventories of goods imported from countries with devaluation-prone currencies. While sterling is exposed to the heavy pressure of hedging by American and other non-resident holders of direct investment or portfolio investment in the U.K., British investors are not allowed to safeguard their interests, at the same time as supporting sterling, by hedging against their overseas investment. In Chapter 29 I propose to argue that such hedging should not only be permitted but in given circumstances it should even be made compulsory.

CHAPTER TEN

LEADS AND LAGS

WE have now reached the most important and the most difficult aspect of our inquiry into the causes of foreign exchange
crises. Although repeated reference was made in earlier chapters to the effect of lengthening the leads in respect of the
imports, and of lengthening the lags in respect of the exports,
of a country whose currency is under a cloud, the subject
certainly deserves much closer and more systematic attention.
It is outside the scope of this book to do full justice to the importance of this aspect of our subject. I sought to accomplish
that task in my book *Leads and Lags: The Main Cause of
Devaluation.*

The term 'leads and lags' is usually employed very loosely
and it is defined in various ways by various authors — indeed
sometimes even by the same author. As I understand it, a
lengthening of leads means that the importing country loses
foreign exchanges sooner, and a lengthening of lags means that
the exporting country gains foreign exchanges later, either by
importing earlier and exporting later, or by paying for imports
earlier and collecting the proceeds of exports later, or by covering the exchange on imports earlier or by covering the exchange
for exports later. What matters is not when the individual
importer actually pays or when the individual exporter actually
receives payment but when the change results in an additional
supply of the importing country's exchange and an additional
demand for the exporting country's exchange, whether spot
or forward.

The full significance of changes in leads and lags among the
causes of foreign exchange crises — or, for that matter, among
the causes of recoveries from foreign exchange crises — is yet
to be realised adequately outside the Treasuries and Central

69

Banks directly concerned.   Their role in foreign exchange
markets is not nearly as well understood as that of speculative
attacks in the conventionally understood sense, or wholesale
withdrawals of foreign balances, or a flight of national capital.
It is not nearly as obvious as an adverse change in the trade
balance, or an increase in Government spending abroad, or
over-investment abroad.   Indeed leads and lags constitute one
of the most neglected and least understood aspects of foreign
exchange.   What Keynes said in 1922 about forward exchange
— that 'there are few financial topics of equal importance which
have received so little discussion or publicity' — is no longer
true about forward exchange but still applies perfectly to leads
and lags.

In his *Foreign Trade Credits and Exchange Reserves*, which is one
of the very few substantial contributions to the subject, Bent
Hansen complains about the absence of statistics relating to
leads and lags and the difficulty of compiling them. He goes on
by saying that the theoretical treatment of the subject consists
mainly of stray remarks of an unsystematic nature.   What was
true when he was writing his book in 1961 is still substantially
true, even though the *Board of Trade Journal* now does publish
some figures.   Hansen's book is concerned mainly with the
'international movement of trade capital', while leads and lags
arising from forward exchange transactions which may not
lead to such movement are only dealt with in detail as a possible profitable alternative device to financing by credits.   Most
other works on foreign exchange, even the otherwise excellent
treatises published recently by Fritz Machlup and Leland B.
Yeager, barely mention the subject.

Yet a lengthening of leads and lags can be a graver threat
to exchanges and to reserves than any other cause of adverse
pressure on the exchanges, with the possible exception of an
intractable trade deficit.   Accountants of business firms are
only too familiar with the striking effect of a change in the
timing of outgoing or incoming payments on the liquidity of
their firms.   Postponement of payments to suppliers, sub-
contractors, the tax collector, etc., by a single week, or a slowing

down of incoming payments by an average of one week, makes a remarkable difference to the size of the firm's bank balance or, as the case may be, to the size of its overdraft. The position is similar in respect of the effect of changes in the timing of foreign payments made or received by a country. Only in the case of a country the difference is on a gigantic scale.

To drive this fact home it should be sufficient to point out the elementary but inadequately realised arithmetical fact that a change in the average leads and lags by a single week is equal to a change of nearly two per cent in the amount of total exports or that of total imports. Since the annual grand total of the U.K.'s foreign trade is roughly £12,000 million, a lengthening of the average leads and lags by one week tends to reduce the reserves by nearly £240 million. As in recent years the British gold and dollar reserve fluctuated very approximately around £1,000 million, if the average of lags for the covering of, or payments for, British exports and the average of leads for the covering of, or payments for, British imports had lengthened by four weeks the resulting deficiency might have exhausted the reserve within twelve months.

Yet the possibility of a lengthening of leads and lags by four weeks does not appear to be too fantastic to be considered. One often hears of instances in which they have been lengthened not by weeks or months but by years. If such instances were characteristic, or even widespread, it would produce a disastrous result. In practice the attitude of individual importers and exporters is indeed very far from being uniform. Although many importers, if they anticipate a devaluation of their currency or a revaluation of the exporting country's currency, lengthen their leads to the maximum limit that is possible under law and under foreign exchange practice, many others make no change at all in their well-established routines.

Until 1967 trade between countries of the Sterling Area was not covered against exchange risk and payments arrangements were unaffected by devaluation scares. It was assumed that a devaluation of sterling would be followed immediately by a devaluation of other Sterling Area currencies. A substantial proportion of U.K. trade could therefore be safely ignored when trying to assess the probable extent of changes in leads and lags. But a great many importers from non-sterling countries and exporters to non-sterling countries also abstained from adjusting their leads and lags, because of the law of inertia or because they did not believe in the likelihood of sterling devaluation.

Commodities which have a futures market of their own can be covered in those markets against the effect of a devaluation on their prices instead of lengthening leads and lags by means of forward exchange transactions or by other means. But in practice most dealers in such commodities take a view on their future prices and only wish to safeguard themselves against the devaluation risk. For this reason they engage in forward exchange transactions if they buy such commodities instead of selling them in the futures market.

At the other extreme there are some industrial firms which are very leads-and-lags minded. Under the influence of acute devaluation scares they may seek to obtain much longer credits, or they cover their payments by forward exchange operations for much longer periods ahead. It seems reasonable to assume that the proportion of trade on which leads and lags were lengthened by several months, and even by years, during recent sterling crises, represented a mere fraction of the total turnover. Otherwise there would have been an irresistible landslide.

In reality forward exchange is very often resorted to irrespective of its cost compared with that of the alternative method of operating leads and lags by credit transactions. Merchants may choose covering by means of forward exchange because they are unable to obtain credits from their banks, or because exchange control prevents their use, or even because they find it much simpler to telephone to the foreign exchange department of their bank to buy or sell exchanges for forward delivery, rather than try to negotiate a bank credit either in the local centre or abroad. It is incomparably simpler and easier to obtain forward facilities for periods exceeding 3 months than to induce the bank manager to depart from routine by granting credits in excess of 3 months.

The choice of the device of covering by means of forward exchange operations regardless of comparative costs, for considerations of easy availability or convenience, plays a very important part in leads and lags. This aspect of the subject, and also the practice of importers hedging against the risk of losses through a fall in the prices of unsold imported goods caused by a devaluation of the exporter's currency, has not been explored according to its merit.

Leads and lags may be changed by either of the two partners in foreign trade transactions, according to the currency in which the goods are invoiced. When sterling is devaluation-prone British importers are inclined to lengthen their leads on goods invoiced in foreign currencies while foreign exporters shorten their lags on goods invoiced in sterling. At the same time British exporters of goods invoiced in foreign exchanges lengthen their lags, while foreign importers of goods invoiced in sterling shorten their leads.

From the point of view of effects of leads and lags on exchange rates, it is not the actual length of the interval between imports or exports and the resulting effect on the foreign exchange situation that matters but changes in the length of that interval. It is the lengthening and shortening of leads and lags that affect supply–demand relationship in the foreign exchange market. But abnormally long leads and lags are a potential source of strength because sooner or later they are likely to be shortened.

Foreign exchange crises are liable to be created or aggravated by a lengthening of leads in the following ways :

(1) Goods invoiced in foreign currencies are imported earlier than usual.

(2) Importers of goods invoiced in foreign currencies who had not been in the habit of covering their foreign exchange requirements in advance decide to cover them.

(3) Those who had been in the habit of covering in advance decide to cover them for longer periods.

(4) Foreign exporters of goods invoiced in the importer's

currency decide to sell forward the proceeds of their
exports instead of awaiting the receipt of the money.

(5) Those who had been in the habit of selling forward
the proceeds decide to sell forward a longer period
ahead.

(6) Importers who had been hedging against the devaluation risk on their inventories — U.K. firms are not permitted to do so — now cease to do so.

(7) Importers obtain shorter credits than before.

(8) Instead of obtaining credit, they have to pay cash.

(9) Instead of being given credit or paying cash they have
to pay in advance.

(10) Importers who had been obtaining credits abroad
finance their imports henceforth with credits obtained
in their own country.

(11) Foreign exporters, instead of financing their exports in
their own country or in a third country, finance them
in the importing country.

(12) Acceptances financing imports, instead of being kept
in the portfolios of banks in the importers' country,
are discounted abroad.

The scope for lengthening the lags is as wide as for lengthening the leads. In so far as leads and lags operated by means
of forward exchange, it is as easy, or as difficult, to buy forward
for longer periods as to sell forward for longer periods.

Foreign exchanges are liable to be affected by a lengthening
of lags in the following ways :

(1) Exports invoiced in foreign currencies are delayed.

(2) Exporters of goods invoiced in foreign currencies dispose of the proceeds of their exports later than before.

(3) Those who had been in the habit of selling the proceeds
forward decide to discontinue that practice.

(4) Foreign importers of goods invoiced in the exporter's
currency, who had been covering their requirements
of that currency in advance, now cease to do so, or
cover for shorter periods.

(5) Foreign importers who have not hitherto hedged against

the devaluation risk on their inventories of imported goods decide to hedge against it.

(6) Foreign importers of goods invoiced in the exporters' currency obtain longer credits than before.

(7) Instead of paying cash they now obtain credit.

(8) Instead of paying in advance they now pay cash.

(9) Exporters or foreign importers who had hitherto obtained credits abroad will obtain credits henceforth in the exporting country's currency.

(10) Acceptances in foreign currencies, instead of being discounted abroad, are kept in the portfolios of the banks in the exporters' country.

It emerges from the above that the length of leads and lags depends on the following circumstances:

(a) The timing of imports and exports.

(b) The terms of payment (whether the goods sold on longer or shorter credit, cash or advance payment).

(c) The covering of the foreign exchange (whether it is covered and if so for how long a period in advance of the date when payment is due).

(d) The choice of the country in which the transactions are financed.

(e) The choice of the currency in which the transactions are financed. Since the development of the Euro-currency markets it has become easier to finance foreign trade in one's own centre in various foreign currencies.

A lengthening of the period for which imports are covered by means of forward exchange transactions does not in itself increase the overall pressure on the exchange, unless it entails the covering of larger amounts of imports. If it only means that the same amount of imports is covered for, say, 6 months instead of 3 months, it may affect the difference between forward rates for 3 and 6 months, but it does not add to the overall pressure on the exchange. What usually happens on such occasions, however, is that importers who had already covered payments due in 3 months now deem it expedient to cover in addition also payments due in 6 months, instead of covering those payments in 3 months' time only. Having covered their June payments in March, they also cover in March the payments due in September. If they wish to maintain the increased length of the leads in June, they will cover their December payments, instead of covering them in September only. In March, when the leads are lengthened, there is additional demand for forward exchanges.

Importers and exporters of goods are not alone in being concerned with leads and lags. Contractors who decide to hedge against an increase of their expenditure abroad as a result of a devaluation of their currency or a revaluation of the currency of the country in which they are to carry out the work contracted for, or who decide to cover the devaluation risk on the payment in foreign currency they are to receive, also contribute towards changing the length of leads and lags. In a broader sense, decisions whether to cover exchange risk on future financial liabilities and claims, and if so for what period, also enter into the picture. Payments arising from invisible imports and exports (travel agencies' expenditure abroad, and even the timing of individual tourists' foreign currency purchases) also tend to affect leads and lags.

The following are the main causes that are liable to influence decisions that affect the practice of leads and lags:

(1) Anticipation of a devaluation or revaluation of a foreign currency or of the local currency.

(2) Changes in practices, commercial or banking.

(3) Changes of the composition of foreign trade.

(4) Availability of forward exchange and Euro-currency facilities.

(5) Relationship between interest parities and forward rates or between long and short interest rates or forward rates.

(6) Delays through exchange control.

(7) Changes in statutory limits for forward covering or for surrendering export proceeds.

(8) Payment delays for commercial reasons.

Anticipation of changes in exchange rates is from the point

of view of exchange crises the most important influence affecting leads and lags. In addition to affecting the timing of imports and exports themselves, it influences the decisions of importers and exporters on the timing of payments and on the foreign exchange transactions involved. This latter is even more important than the timing of trade transactions and of payments. It is often impracticable or inexpedient to hasten imports or to delay imports for the sake of benefiting by the expected change in the exchange rate. Terms of payment, too, are often difficult to alter, if they are fixed by custom or by contract. On the other hand, importers and exporters can always cover in advance by means of forward exchange transactions up to the statutory limit — in so far as the required long forward facilities are available to them — or delay the disposal of the foreign currency proceeds, again up to the statutory limit, without having to disturb existing arrangements with customers or suppliers.

A lengthening of leads and lags is apt to be of decisive importance to the outcome of a currency scare. It is known to have been of decisive importance in Britain in 1949 when it enforced a devaluation of the pound, even though exchange control prevented speculation and capital movements.

Businessmen who lengthen leads and lags during currency scares are often accused of engaging in speculation against the currency. Yet there is a strong case for importers and exporters to safeguard themselves against losses through a devaluation. For one thing they can never be sure whether their rivals cover against the devaluation risk. If so, importers who omit that precaution are placed in a position to undersell them if the exporters' currency is devalued. There is some moral justification also for exporters to lengthen their lags, if their goods are invoiced in a revaluation-prone currency.

Changes in practices in regard to terms of payment may occur independently of any speculative anticipation of changes in exchange rates, in the following circumstances:

(1) When a sellers' market changes into a buyers' market, or *vice versa*. In a buyers' market importers are in a position

to influence, if not dictate, the terms of payment owing
to fierce competition of exporters to meet their wishes.
In a sellers' market exporters are in a position to impose
or influence terms of payment.

(2) Government pressure for an export drive, or official
stimulus in the form of guaranteed long-term credits
induces exporters to lengthen lags in order to compete
with the terms of payment offered by their foreign rivals.

(3) Changes in the relative degree of liquidity of exporters
and importers or their respective bankers are liable to
affect their credit terms.

(4) Changes in the extent of confidence in the solvency of
buyers may induce exporters to change their terms of
payment.

(5) Changes in the composition of foreign trade. For instance the reduction of the relative importance of British
textile exports and the increase in the relative importance
of capital goods exports have greatly increased the length
of average lags for all exports, because capital goods are
sold on the basis of much longer credits than textiles.

Altogether the world trend is towards longer lags — which
of course means shorter leads viewed from the angle of importers
— because imports tend to consist increasingly of capital goods.
This should mean a secular trend towards longer lags. That
trend is mitigated, however, by the decline in the self-sufficiency
of industrial countries in raw materials and food, because it
influences leads and lags in the opposite sense, since raw materials and food are paid on delivery or on a short-term credit
basis, or, in given circumstances, they may be covered in their
own market for commodity futures and not in the forward
exchange market.

The improvement of forward exchange facilities for longer
periods and the development of Euro-currency markets for
long maturities tend to lengthen leads and lags. The relative
levels of interest rates in importing and exporting countries
and in third countries, or in Euro-currencies, and their relation
to forward rates, influence decisions in which markets and in

which currencies imports and exports should be financed. This highly technical point is discussed in detail in my *Dynamic Theory of Forward Exchange* and in my *Euro-Dollar System*. Discrepancies between long and short interest rates, and even more between long and short forward rates, may also exert some influence on leads and lags.

Exchange control in importing countries is liable to lengthen leads for importers and lags for exporters, because of the delays in payments. External liabilities might even be completely blocked for long periods. During the 'thirties the world-wide adoption of exchange controls lengthened lags very considerably and accounted to a large extent for foreign exchange crises in creditor countries. In Britain in 1957 the ban on re-financing credits shortened the effective lags considerably on a fair proportion of exports.

Exchange controls are often applied to prevent a lengthening of leads and lags beyond a certain limit. In a number of countries there are statutory limits to the length of time up to which importers are entitled to cover their liabilities, also to the length of time up to which exporters are entitled to retain the proceeds of their exports. Although a high proportion of importers and exporters do not avail themselves of their right to the full, any changes in the time limits are liable to affect average leads and lags. The British time limit for forward covering of import requirements is 6 months, but it is reckoned from the arrival of the last consignment of goods or from the time limit of the import licence. This means that if goods are ordered for delivery in, say, two years, the importer is entitled to cover the exchange for $2\frac{1}{2}$ years. But forward facilities for such distant maturities are only available to favoured clients.

Receipts from exports are often delayed as a result of slow payment by foreign importers. Debtors in some countries have a reputation for slow payment and exporters are often not in a sufficiently strong bargaining position to insist on cash payment or advance payment. In many instances, however, delays of payment result in such insistence and to a resulting shortening of lags.

One of the ways in which leads and lags are apt to lengthen is by businessmen becoming more forward-exchange minded. This institutional change means that an increasing number of importers tend to cover their foreign exchange requirements well in advance and many foreign exporters dispose of their devaluation-prone currencies well in advance.

A lengthening of leads and lags tends to affect exchanges in the same way as a decline in exports or an increase in imports, at any rate during the process while leads and lags are actually being lengthened. It changes supply–demand relationship in the market to the detriment of the currency concerned. If the forward rate is supported against the effect of leads and lags, then instead of losing reserve the authorities increase their forward exchange commitments. If in the absence of official support a counterpart is forthcoming in the market at a price, the reserve is affected indirectly because a depreciation of the forward rate leads to outward arbitrage.

The possibility of an aggravation of foreign exchange crises through a lengthening of leads and lags has added considerably to the uncertainty of the foreign exchange situation and prospects, precisely because of the multiplicity of causes for which leads and lags are liable to lengthen. Moreover, they are statistically incalculable. While even trade figures contain a strong element of uncertainty, they do give a fair aide of the nature and extent of changes, although there is a time lag during which it is largely a matter of guesswork. There are more or less dependable statistics on certain invisible trade items, terms of trade, capital movements, etc. The least calculable items are speculation and leads and lags.

In order to beable to judge the situation it is essential to have an idea of the causes of foreign exchange crises. It is of the utmost importance that the authorities, and also critics of the official policies, should be able to form an opinion about the trend of changes in leads and lags, even if it is impossible to ascertain statistically the extent of such changes. Each bank has an approximate idea about the way its clients change their leads and lags, and such information as they possess should be pooled. It would be too much to expect banks to include in their returns concrete figures about the extent of the changes, because such an exercise would involve immense clerical labour. But the Board of Trade initiated in 1967 a statistical series on the amounts of outstanding international trade credits. It is based on returns made by 2,300 firms in respect of credits they granted to foreign importers and on returns made by 1,595 firms in respect of credits they receive from foreign exporters. The material is far from ideal but it is a good beginning and has promising possibilities. Technically it is not impossible to compile statistics also in respect of forward covering by importers and exporters. But it would involve a great deal of clerical labour. Moreover, the picture changes from day to day — indeed almost from hour to hour — to such extent that figures relating to any one day (such as the last business day of each year) might be unrepresentative, besides being completely out of date and therefore misleading by the time they are issued. Even so, such statistics would be better than nothing. Anyhow, it would be a great improvement on the existing attempts at deductions about leads and lags reached on the basis of changes in the residual item in the balance of payments.

Another extremely difficult task would be to assess the extent to which changes in foreign short-term assets and liabilities of banks are the results of leads and lags by their clients. As for trying to assess the extent to which imports and exports themselves have been put forward or delayed, it is bordering on the impossible. Even so, an effort should be made to find a basis for intelligent estimates.

After all, it is to the interest of all sections of the community that foreign exchange policy should be well-informed, and it cannot be well-informed unless the authorities can form an idea how leads and lags are going.

It cannot be a matter of indifference to the monetary authorities whether pressure on the exchange is primarily due to leads and lags or to other causes. From the point of view of the intensity and duration of a foreign exchange crisis leads and lags are probably more dangerous than pure speculation, or investment-hedging, or withdrawals of foreign funds, or even flight of national capital, precisely because the potential extent of additional pressure due to leads and lags is much greater. As Britain discovered at her cost in 1949, such additional pressure is liable to deplete the reserve even if there is no free foreign exchange market and if all transactions connected with foreign trade have to go through the hands of the authorities. It seems reasonable to suppose that during the earlier phases of the crisis of 1949 Sir Stafford Cripps and his advisers failed to realise the extent to which leads and lags were able to force the Government's hands; hence his repeated categorical denials of any intention to devalue. Had he been aware of the extent to which the possibility of maintaining sterling's stability depended on leads and lags he might have hesitated to commit himself quite so firmly to the policy which he was fated to abandon eventually.

One of the causes of the dynamism of leads and lags lies in the fact that the system is liable to be practised not only by importers and exporters of the country concerned but also by importers and exporters abroad who are buyers or sellers of its goods. As a general rule the national currency is trusted to a higher degree at home than abroad, especially by nationals of countries which had experienced no runaway inflation. Distrustful foreign importers and exporters trading with Britain and with the Sterling Area are not handicapped by British and Sterling Area exchange controls in their leading and lagging operations to the same extent as British or Sterling Area importers and exporters. Their leads and lags are apt to be, therefore, even more important than those of residents in the U.K. and in the Sterling Area.

The absolute and relative importance of leads and lags among causes of foreign exchange crises necessarily has its ups and downs, but it seems probable that in the long run it will increase, largely owing to the increasing extent to which merchants tend to become foreign exchange minded. Today a much higher proportion of U.K. importers and exporters think in terms of covering exchange risks than before the War, if only because a higher proportion of U.K. foreign trade is now invoiced in foreign currencies. Facilities for forward covering have also greatly improved, especially for long periods for which there were virtually no facilities before the War. Yet forward covering of a substantial and increasing proportion of foreign trade for periods of years might lengthen average leads and lags to an intolerable extent during acute foreign exchange crises. The extent of the fluctuations of leads and lags might then become incomparably more disturbing than it is in our days. However that may be, we have to envisage that possibility.

Of course whenever confidence in the maintenance of parities returns the resulting shortening of leads and lags, as indeed the reversal of other influences making for foreign exchange crises, produces a most welcome effect on the exchange concerned. Such benefits do not adequately compensate, however, for the disturbing effects of the leads and lags during waves of distrust.

The importance of the role of leads and lags in causing and aggravating foreign exchange crises is likely to be realised increasingly, not only by official opinion and expert opinion, but even by the general public. Today the gnomes who speculate against sterling or who withdraw their sterling balances are still popularly regarded as the villains of the piece. But there is a growing tendency on the part of economically illiterate politicians to accuse merchants of increasing our difficulties by trying to safeguard their legitimate interests. It is all the more important that there should be a correct understanding of the problems involved.

CHAPTER ELEVEN

OUTWARD ARBITRAGE

TRANSFERS of funds abroad from a centre whose currency is under selling pressure, undertaken for the sake of higher yield obtainable in the other centres through covered interest arbitrage, constitute yet another cause of foreign exchange crises. They tend to aggravate crises because the pressure is in addition to that due to the creation of short positions for various purposes. Apart altogether from the heavy drain on the reserve due to operations by speculators and others who distrust the currency in question, there is also a loss of reserves due to operations by arbitrageurs who do not distrust that currency and do not wish to sell out their holdings of it or go short in it. They swap their holdings temporarily into the currency of the centre which offers higher yield on short-term investment, allowing for the cost of the swap. What happens is that those who distrust the currency in question provide opportunities for outward arbitrage by causing the forward discount to widen, while those who trust the currency take advantage of the arbitrage profit possibility thus created for their benefit.

The flow of funds through interest arbitrage depends on the relative level of interest rates and on the extent to which the yield from the interest differentials is reduced or increased by the swap margin. Interest rates are usually higher in a centre whose currency is devaluation-prone. But in normal conditions the distrust in that currency results in a wide discount in its forward quotation, so that, if we allow for the profit on the swap, the low interest rates prevailing in the foreign centre offer a higher combined yield.

In the absence of intervention in forward exchanges selling pressure on a forward exchange widens the forward discount to such an extent that, in spite of the high interest rates resulting from the defensive policies of its authorities, it becomes profitable to transfer funds abroad. The extent to which residents are able to take advantage of this is limited by exchange control. In Britain only banks are entitled to engage in outward interest arbitrage without licence, and the total amount of their commitments in such transactions is limited. On the other hand, nonresidents are at liberty to withdraw all their liquid holdings of sterling whenever they choose to do so because the funds can be employed more profitably in other centres.

In the past, before exchange control was adopted, pressure on the spot exchange was aggravated through outward arbitrage by residents and also by non-residents operating with the aid of money borrowed in the centre whose currency was under pressure. Between the wars the Governments concerned were doing their best during foreign exchange crises to dissuade their banks from lending for that purpose, but their only effective means for preventing it in the absence of exchange control was by raising their interest rates and tightening credit conditions. This was done on many occasions between the wars, and it was largely responsible for increasing interest rates and credit squeezes in countries whose currencies were under pressure. More often than not, higher interest rates further widened the discount on their forward exchange, thereby cancelling out the effect of high interest rates.

In countries where exchange control now prevents residents from engaging in outward interest arbitrage and where banks are not permitted to grant credits to non-residents for that purpose the extent to which outward arbitrage can contribute towards aggravating foreign exchange crises is limited. Even so, a widening of profit margins on the transactions usually succeeds somehow in attracting additional funds into such operations, especially funds owned by non-residents.

One of the objects of extensive official support to the forward rate of currency under pressure is to keep down the discount, thereby making it less profitable, or entirely unprofitable, to engage in outward interest arbitrage. To the extent to which official selling of forward exchanges, by keeping down forward

D

margins, prevents outward arbitrage, it substitutes an increase in official forward commitments for a loss of reserves. This is one of the arguments used in favour of official support to the forward exchange, about which more will be said in Chapter 22.

How does outward arbitrage affect the exchange of the losing centre? The operation may consist of buying the foreign spot exchange against the sale of the forward exchange. In other words, holders of sterling buy dollars for a fixed period and re-sell them against sterling for the end of that period. In the absence of official intervention they have to find holders of dollars who are prepared to acquire sterling for the same period. The difficulty about that is that at a time when it is profitable to transfer funds from London to New York for covered interest arbitrage a transfer of funds from New York to London for that purpose would usually involve a loss. Profit could only be earned on uncovered interest arbitrage, but that would create a long position in sterling and would involve devaluation risk. On some occasions it is possible to make a profit through inward as well as outward arbitrage, when certain interest rates in London — such as loans to Local Authorities — are so high that it more than offsets the cost of the swap.

But pressure on forward sterling can originate also through speculative selling on non-resident account, which is unlimited. For this reason covered outward arbitrage by British banks may not be able to provide the full counterpart to speculative selling of forward sterling. On the other hand, in spite of exchange control, non-residents are now able to continue engaging in outward arbitrage after having exhausted their own resources, with the aid of borrowed Euro-sterling. This is an instance to show that the development of Euro-currency markets has increased not only facilities for speculation but also facilities for outward arbitrage.

Intervention in forward exchanges, by keeping swap margins at a level at which outward arbitrage is unprofitable, can prevent or keep down losses of reserves through arbitrage. But this end can only be achieved at the cost of encouraging speculation, hedging and prolongation of leads and lags by reducing the cost of such operations. It is of course open to argument whether or not the psychological effect of a wide discount on the forward exchange outweighs the effect of the reduced cost of the operations.

The controversy over unlimited support of the forward exchange of a devaluation-prone currency in face of basic disequilibrium has been effectively settled by the circumstances of sterling's disastrous devaluation in 1967. It conclusively proved that in the long run defence by means of unlimited intervention to keep down the discount on forward sterling was doomed to be ineffective. The mistake cost Britain a loss which was variously estimated at between £300 million and £500 million. It was a free gift to speculators who were enabled to maintain short positions at a negligible cost. Even two years after the devaluation a substantial proportion of the Bank of England's short position in dollars created before November 1967 still remained open, constituting a burden on sterling in addition to the debts owed to the IMF and to foreign Central Banks. Such is the price the country has to pay for an error of judgment in the choice of the device with which to defend a currency under pressure.

PART TWO

INDIRECT CAUSES OF CRISES

CHAPTER TWELVE

INFLATION

HITHERTO we have been dealing with the principal direct causes of foreign exchange crises. The present chapter and the four subsequent chapters examine the more fundamental indirect causes that produce their adverse effects on exchanges through the intermediary of one or several of the direct causes. It is essential to realise the importance of these indirect causes when trying to deal with foreign exchange crises, because attempts to deal with their direct causes without taking their indirect causes into consideration are not likely to produce satisfactory results. For instance, as we propose to show in Chapter 19, efforts to reduce a trade balance deficit through an export drive need not produce results if the main basic cause of the deficit is inflationary overfull-employment.

One fact emerges clearly from the preceding chapters — that much more often than not inflation is the basic cause of foreign exchange crises. So long as the domestic economy is at equilibrium the defence of the national currency seldom presents great difficulties. When the economy is deflationary the national currency is usually subject to buying pressure, unless, of course, the economies of other leading countries are even more deflationary. But when the economy is inflationary the exchange is subject to adverse pressure that is liable to develop into a crisis, always provided that the economies of other countries are not even more inflationary.

If all countries inflated simultaneously and to approximately the same extent, there would be no reason why inflation should affect the relative value of their currencies in terms of each other. But although the secular world trend is distinctly inflationary, the degree of inflation at any given moment is apt to vary considerably from country to country. Indeed, from time to time, some countries might keep aloof altogether from the world trend and might even experience periods of deflation, while other countries might be well ahead of the world trend of inflation. Such discrepancies cause disequilibrium between their price levels leading to buying or selling pressure on the exchanges. If the extent of the discrepancies is sufficiently marked the resulting depreciating trend of the exchanges of countries with a relatively advanced inflation develops into a foreign exchange crisis.

Inflation of every kind was at one time or other responsible for foreign exchange crises. The best-known early instance of inflation that had affected foreign exchanges was the sharp rise in the supply of specie in Spain during the 16th century as a result of the heavy influx of gold and silver from the New World. The exchange value of the maravedi was strongly affected by the inflated quantity of metallic currency in circulation. It is of course impossible to ascertain with any degree of certainty to what extent the depreciation of the maravedi was due to this inflation — in addition to its depreciation due to successive debasements — and to what extent it was due to the heavy military expenditure abroad referred to in Chapter 4. But there can be no doubt that, had it not been for the effect of rising prices and, even more, for the demoralising effect of inflation on Spanish production and consumption, a larger part of the military expenditure overseas might have been covered by exports, or at any rate the effect of that expenditure would not have been aggravated to the same extent by that of a perennially adverse trade balance.

There are many instances of foreign exchange crises resulting from paper-money inflation. Best known among them are the effect of the *assignats* inflation during the French revolution and the German mark inflation during and after the first World War. But the inflationary effects of unrestricted use of the printing press on the foreign exchange situation were clearly discernible in many other instances, notably during the 19th century in Russia and Austria, also in many Latin American countries. Between the two wars, especially during the early and middle 'twenties, most of the former belligerent countries experienced recurrent foreign exchange crises as a result of financing Budgetary deficits with the aid of the printing press. In reconstruction schemes carried out under the auspices of the League of Nations stability of exchanges was achieved through checking paper-money inflation, mostly with the aid of international loans that gave the Governments concerned a breathing space to enable them to balance their Budgets.

In a modern financially advanced country the direct and indirect causes or symptoms of inflation are very numerous. The following are some of the most important amongst them :

(1) Increase in the note issue.
(2) Expansion in the volume of bank credit.
(3) Expansion in the volume of hire-purchase credits.
(4) Budgetary deficit.
(5) Increase in spendings by Local Authorities.
(6) Increase in the volume of short-term Government borrowing.
(7) Increase in capital investment by industries.
(8) Decline in savings.
(9) Increase in wages in excess of productivity.
(10) Decline in the output.

It is a widely held view that in advanced countries the increase in the volume of notes is merely one of the manifestations of inflation and never its cause, as the increased note requirements caused by inflation have to be satisfied. In reality even in advanced countries such as Britain a high proportion of inflation assumes the form of payments in notes, so that the increase of the note circulation is a cause as well as a symptom of inflation. But in advanced countries the expansion in the volume of credit plays a much more important part. It is not only bank credits that matter but also credits by financial intermediaries, especially by hire-purchase finance houses. An increase in their borrowings and lendings tends to increase the velocity of circulation of bank credits. In other words, the same amount of bank money is used more frequently.

Budgetary deficits are among the most obvious causes of

D 2

inflation leading to crises. For instance, the foreign exchange market during the inter-war period adopted the habit of judging the prospects of the franc mainly according to its assessment of the Budgetary prospects in France. For a long time it was widely believed that if the Government was able to cover the deficit by borrowing instead of resorting to the printing press the inflationary effect of its deficit is neutralised. But under the British system if the Budgetary deficit is covered through the issue of Treasury bills the resulting increase in the banks' liquid resources provides a basis for an expansion of bank credit several times its amount. The experience of the first World War in Germany and other countries showed that even the covering of the Budgetary deficit by long-term borrowing is no safeguard against its inflationary effect.

Inflation due to borrowing by Local Authorities is yet another indirect cause of foreign exchange crisis. In Britain during 1965–66 it was one of the many causes why the measures adopted in defence of sterling were ineffective. Although the immediate effect of borrowing with the aid of Euro-dollars converted into sterling was favourable to sterling, the spending spree that the proceeds financed was largely responsible for the increasing overload on the economy, leading to persistent recurrence of sterling scares.

Even though the long-term effect of increased capital investment by industries, as indeed of productive capital investment by the Government, is favourable, its immediate effect is inflationary. If it exceeds the volume of savings available for financing it is liable to affect the balance of payments and the exchange. The popular observation that sterling is in difficulties because Britain is trying to do too much in too short a time is based on the inflationary effect of over-investment even if it be for productive purposes. A similar effect is liable to be caused by a decline in savings, or its inadequate expansion, not only because it means an inflationary increase in consumer demand but also because industrial investment, not being covered by new savings, results in an immediate net increase in demand.

By far the most important cause of sterling crises during the post-war period has been the increase in unearned wages — that is, increase of wages in excess of the increase in productivity. Even in instances in which the rise in prices had been originally a justification for part of the wage increases, the absence of any adequate resistance to wage increases was responsible for the vicious spiral in the course of which increase of wages caused by increase of prices is followed by further increase in prices. It was too easy to concede costly wage increases and to pass them on to the consumer.

Likewise, the relative decline in the output — that is, the inadequate extent to which wage increases were followed by increases in the output — produced inflationary effects. It also had a more direct effect on sterling, because owing to the increased proportion of the output absorbed by domestic demand there was not enough exportable surplus, and there was not sufficient inducement to export, because it was too easy to sell the output at home.

An expansion in the output is not inflationary in the long run because the inflationary effect of the additional cost of production paid out in the process is offset by the increased output. But there is always a time lag between paying for equipment, raw materials, wages, etc., and mopping up the resulting additional purchasing power through an increased supply of goods. That time lag is relatively brief in the case of additional consumer goods which can be produced within existing capacity. It is longer if producing capacity has to be expanded in order to achieve an increased output, even if the capital goods required can be produced within existing capacity. It is the longest of all in the case of capital goods the increase of whose production necessitates an increase of productive capacity. In the case of non-productive capital goods the purchasing power created in the course of their production is not mopped up at all in the form of additional supplies, but it is mopped up through additional taxation or through additional saving.

The inflationary effect of the time lag between input and

output does affect exchanges, and unduly rapid growth tends to be accompanied by exchange depreciation that is liable to develop into a crisis. It has become a widely adopted deliberate policy in a number of countries to risk such a crisis, or at any rate to allow the defences of exchange stability to weaken as a result of loss of reserves, for the sake of accelerated growth. Indeed this 'growth-hysteria' has become one of the major basic causes of foreign exchange crises. Considerations of security and stability are often cheerfully sacrificed for the sake of speeding up non-stop expansion. Foreign exchange difficulties due to this cause occurred in most Western European countries at one time or other since the war, though some of them did not allow the adverse trend to develop into an acute crisis. Britain provided a flagrant instance of a country whose expansionary ambitions led to frequent foreign exchange crises during the post-war period, even though the actual extent of expansion achieved left much to be desired, because of the low productivity of labour.

By far the most important cause of post-war exchange crises in Britain has been, however, inflation due to overfull-employment. Determination not to tolerate a return of large-scale unemployment experienced between the wars caused the pendulum to swing to the opposite direction. During most of the post-war period Britain suffered from acute overfull-employment, even if the highly unsatisfactory statistics of unfilled vacancies did not show it adequately. As a result of acute scarcity of labour, trade unions were placed in a position virtually to dictate their terms. Wage increases were all the time ahead of the increase in productivity, and the difference was made up in an inflationary increase of prices. Although the number of working hours lost through strikes was, during a number of years, smaller than in many other industrial countries, this was because British employers preferred to yield to wage demands rather than risk strikes through attempts to resist them.

Labour conditions, by generating inflation, were responsible for the frequent sterling crises for the following reasons:

(1) They caused costs to rise.

(2) They increased domestic demand, thereby reducing surpluses available for export.

(3) This increase in domestic demand made it unessential for industrial firms to exert themselves to sell abroad.

(4) It also increased demand for imported goods.

(5) Unsatisfactory productive effort of labour made for long delivery dates.

(6) Frequency of official and unofficial strikes, go-slow, etc. made delivery dates uncertain and undependable.

From time to time there were strikes in major industries that gravely affected the production and supply of exports. Or there were strikes by a handful of key employees which were able to paralyse entire industries. In the foreign exchange market the labour situation came to be watched closely. Any obviously excessive wage increases and any major industrial disputes, or even industrial action other than strikes, gave rise to a fresh wave of pessimism, and sterling came under pressure.

Apart altogether from strikes and wage increases the output was usually unsatisfactory, owing to tactics of go-slow in order to earn more overtime pay. Restrictive practices resulted in the employment of an excessive number of hands, a high proportion of which was quite unproductive. Wildcat strikes at the flimsiest excuses made for uncertainty and fears of such strikes undermined industrial discipline.

Even during attempts to check inflation the most that was ever achieved was to slow down the increase of unearned wages, at a time when the output was either stagnant or was actually falling, and when profits and dividends were down.

These conditions alone would have provided ample justification for distrust in sterling. They prevented the accumulation of a really strong reserve throughout the whole post-war period. The British tradition of maintaining the stability of sterling on a shoestring prevented or delayed defensive action until the reserves threatened to decline to danger level.

Cost inflation affected sterling because in many lines British firms became unable to compete with their foreign rivals. It is true, in many industries wages in Britain were actually lower than in a number of other industrial countries. But while in the U.S. and on the Continent workers put in a full day's work for their pay, in Britain restrictive practices and the general attitude of workers towards their employers and towards the community kept the output per man-hour low, so that lower wages did not prevent costs from rising above those of countries in which higher wages were paid for more work. British exports lost markets and foreign firms were able to undersell their British rivals in certain goods even in the British home market.

Demand inflation, too, contributed towards weakening sterling's position, precisely because it mopped up too much of Britain's output and because it resulted in increased imports.

CHAPTER THIRTEEN

POLITICAL CAUSES

ACCORDING to a much-quoted remark made by Baron Louis, French Finance Minister of the Restoration, a Finance Minister can only maintain satisfactory financial conditions if his Government maintains satisfactory political conditions. Unsatisfactory political conditions are liable to create or accentuate various direct causes of foreign exchange crises. Speculation against a currency is very often due to fears of unfavourable political developments of a kind that would react on the economic situation and would jeopardise monetary stability. Such threats may arise either in the sphere of domestic politics or in that of international politics.

In the sphere of domestic politics the following developments might lead to foreign exchange crises:

(1) The advent of a Government with unsound economic, financial or monetary policies, especially one in whose scheme of things stability of the national currency has a low priority.

(2) The advent of a Government hostile to business interests.

(3) The adoption of prohibitive taxation.

(4) Unstable Government.

(5) Fears of the advent of an even worse Government emerging from the next election.

(6) Unpopularity of the Government, leading to resistance to its measures.

(7) Threat of civil war.

(8) Actual civil war.

A Government that earns the distrust of bankers and businessmen at home and abroad is liable to face frequent pressure on the exchange. Against such a background relatively moderate adverse influences are liable to produce an effect on exchanges that is out of proportion to their intrinsic destructive force. This is partly because the foreign exchange market assumes, rightly or wrongly, that the Government concerned would be unwilling to forgo its objectives for the sake of maintaining the stability of its exchange.

Hostility of a Government to business and investor interests is liable to cause an outflow of capital, domestic and foreign. The adoption of class-war legislation and 'soak-the-rich' taxation, or the administration of the country in a sense hostile to business, is deemed to be detrimental to progress and stability and generates a widespread feeling of pessimism in the foreign exchange market.

Prohibitive class-war taxation is liable to affect the exchanges through discouraging the inflow of foreign money and stimulating its outflow, through leading to a flight of domestic capital, and through reducing incentive, thereby causing a decline in productivity or at any rate its inadequate increase compared with rival nations. Whenever some new measure of this kind is adopted, its psychological effect is liable to cause an attack on the exchange even before it could actually produce its material effect.

Instability of a Government is always a cause for concern in the foreign exchange market. Frequent changes of Government, such as we witnessed in France between the wars and again after the end of the second World War until the advent of General de Gaulle, make for weak exchanges. Conversely, a perennial weakness of an exchange and a frequent recurrence of acute foreign exchange crises is liable to contribute strongly towards the instability of the Government in office. Frequent Government changes are always a cause for concern, for during their brief tenure of office Governments are not in a very good position to restore stability and confidence. They don't dare to adopt the unpopular measures needed for strengthening the exchange, for fear of jeopardising their position and prospects.

Unstable Governments may mean frequent elections. Approaching elections are often a source of anxiety to the foreign exchange market, for no matter how unsatisfactory the to a remarkably high degree during their wars, and they were able to restore normal conditions soon after the end of these wars. The experience of the two World Wars was of course quite another story.

The Suez war in 1956, by closing the direct route for Middle East oil to Britain, might easily have caused a first-rate sterling crisis had it not been for the basic strength of sterling. The withdrawal of British forces from East of Suez is certain to cause such a crisis as a result of the loss of invisible exports earned from British investments of some £1,200 million in Southern Asia and of the withdrawal of Arab oil-producing countries from the Sterling Area.

The way in which the French disturbances of 1968 converted one of the strongest currencies into one of the weakest currencies in a matter of weeks is an outstanding instance illustrating the importance of the political factor among the influences liable to cause foreign exchange crises.

It appears from the above that in given circumstances political influences are liable to overshadow economic influences among the causes of foreign exchange crises.

CHAPTER FOURTEEN

DEVELOPMENTS ABROAD

FOREIGN exchange crises need not always originate in the countries whose exchange come under pressure. In many instances they are the victims of circumstances which they are not in a position to control. The weakness of their exchanges may be due to policies or developments in foreign countries. The following is a list of some of the most important of such developments:

(1) Bank rate increases abroad, or Euro-currency rate increases, leading to an outflow of funds.

(2) Booms on foreign Stock Exchanges, attracting capital.

(3) Deflation in foreign countries.

(4) Devaluation of foreign currencies.

(5) Competitive currency depreciation race.

(6) Slumps in foreign countries.

(7) Changes in import requirements abroad.

(8) Exchange controls abroad.

(9) Import controls abroad.

(10) Currency chaos causing an increase of risk on foreign trade.

(11) Wholesale defaults of foreign debtors.

Increases in interest rates abroad, unless compensated by a corresponding adjustment of forward rates, are liable to cause pressure on the foreign exchanges through causing an outflow of funds by holders who want to benefit by the higher yield obtainable abroad. A similar effect is liable to be produced by increases in Euro-currency rates. Although in theory forward rates are supposed to adjust themselves to changes in their interest parities, this may be prevented by persistent one-sided pressure on forward rates or by official intervention in forward exchanges.

even for merchants in a country with a stable exchange to safeguard themselves against losses through exchange rate fluctuations by means of forward exchange transactions. The forward exchange market might become saturated if, owing to the increase in the demand for forward exchange facilities, the limits of most banks for accepting most other names for forward exchange contracts are reached. Such a situation developed in the early 'thirties. The possibility of its recurrence has been greatly increased by official intervention in the forward exchange market on a large scale during recent years. That possibility is liable to become a near-certainty if a system of floating exchanges should ever be adopted. The volume of foreign trade and other international transactions which give rise to forward exchange covering is now a great deal larger than it was during the pre-war period of floating exchanges. Exchange control fears might also deter banks from committing themselves too heavily.

Large-scale bankruptcies abroad, or a moratorium abroad, are liable to imperil the stability of exchanges. As far as the defaulting debtor's exchange is concerned, it would prevent a depreciation — hence the pre-war term 'gold insolvency standard', meaning the maintenance of stability through non-payment of external debts. But the exchanges of creditor countries would be affected, not only through the resulting loss of foreign exchange but also through the resulting wave of distrust. Major failures would give rise to anticipation of more failures or of a moratorium, which is liable to induce foreign holders of the creditor country's currency to play for safety.

This risk to exchange stability through defaulted debts has greatly increased as a result of the creation and expansion of the international markets in Euro-currencies, in which the same deposit is apt to be lent and re-lent a number of times and a chain of claims is thereby created. The strength of such a chain depends on the strength of its weakest link, and one default might lead to a series of defaults, not so much owing to the inability of borrowers to meet their financial obligation owing to default by their debtors as owing to the unwillingness of their monetary authorities to authorise the exchange required for meeting claims in the absence of payments by the defaulting debtors. In 1963, following on several defaults in Euro-currencies, the Bank of France warned the French banks not to depend on the granting of such licences for foreign exchange if they should come to need them owing to defaults by their own foreign debtors.

Although any currency is liable to be exposed to adverse developments abroad described in this chapter, this possibility must not be used as an excuse for adopting a fatalistic attitude. It is easy and cheap to claim that a country whose exchange has come under pressure through developments abroad is in no way to blame for circumstances over which its authorities have no control. For in most instances the country concerned has the remedies in its own hand. It should be willing and able to deflate at short notice whenever this should become necessary in face of an unexpected foreign exchange crisis of a magnitude that rules out the possibility of meeting it through running down the reserves or through temporary borrowing abroad. So long as a country pursues sound policies that inspire confidence abroad, showing an obvious contrast in its favour, it should be able to ride the storm.

What matters is that we should never allow disequilibrium to develop in our economy. As soon as symptoms appear indicating an overload, the necessary corrective measures should be applied without delay. More will be said about this in Part III. Here let it be sufficient to say that while a small country might be landed into a crisis through developments in larger countries, the larger countries which are not economic satellites of other countries should be well in a position to safeguard themselves against foreign exchange crises caused by developments abroad. But if advanced deflation abroad makes it necessary to administer an unduly heavy dose of deflation for the sake of avoiding a foreign exchange crisis then it might become preferable to devalue.

CHAPTER FIFTEEN

STRUCTURAL CHANGES

WE saw in the last chapter that structural changes abroad may lead to foreign exchange crises through their effect on the export trade of other countries. Structural changes nearer home are liable to produce a similar effect. The absence of adjustments of the economy of a country in order to meet fundamental changes in requirements comes under the definition of structural changes in a negative sense.

The following are the main types of positive structural changes in the domestic economy of a nation that are liable to react unfavourably on its exchange :

(1) Deterioration of producing capacity.
(2) Rise in the standard of living without a corresponding increase in production.
(3) Increase in the population without a corresponding increase in production.
(4) Decline in the willingness or capacity of a country to devote adequate efforts to the maintenance and increase of its foreign markets.
(5) Decline of facilities available for financing exports.
(6) Deterioration of the quality of exportable goods, or absence of their improvement to conform to changing requirements.

Prominent among institutional changes that endanger the exchange is deterioration of producing capacity. It may be the result of war or civil war or some major calamity such as an earthquake or a flood. Or it may come about through a gradual process of deterioration, due to failure to modernise or even to maintain the equipment. In the sphere of agricultural production it may be the result of a decline in efficiency due to a heavy influx of foreign products, or to land reform, etc. The transport equipment of a country may have been allowed to deteriorate. In the sphere of industrial production a structural deterioration could be the result of a far-reaching loosening of industrial discipline or of a marked decline in the employees' willingness to put in an honest day's work for their pay, or through a decline in managerial initiative or efficiency. National production may be affected through an exhaustion of natural resources — minerals, oil, timber, etc. — on which the country had depended for balancing its foreign trade.

A rise in the standard of living is liable to alter the entire pattern of consumption to an extent that amounts to a structural change. Goods which the bulk of the population could not hitherto afford to consume are henceforth sold in the domestic market instead of being available for export. For instance, meat or wheat which was formerly exported is now consumed in the country. An increase in the non-productive population of a country leads to a decline in its exports of food and raw materials. An increase in the number of those with higher incomes means that luxury trades which hitherto produced for exports now produce for the home market. Even if the output does not decline, a rise in the standard of living or an increase of the population reduces the exporting capacity of a country unless it corresponds to an increase in the output.

A decline in the willingness or ability of a country to make the necessary effort to export is a structural change with highly damaging effect on its foreign exchange position. Such a state of affairs is liable to arise through an uninterrupted increase in the absorbing capacity of the domestic markets which makes it too tempting for producers and merchants to neglect their foreign markets.

If as a result of structural changes in the banking system or through basic changes in Government policies — such as for instance a curtailment of officially guaranteed export credit facilities — there is a decline in the facilities available for financing export trade it is liable to affect exports and the exchange.

Deterioration of workmanship is yet another structural

change liable to react on the exchange of a country that
depends on high-quality exports. In view of the world-wide
rising trend of the standard of living in the advanced countries,
this cause is liable to play an increasingly important part in
foreign exchange crises. In a negative sense, failure to keep
up with the world trend of improving the quality of goods is
liable to produce the same effect.

Some difficulties created in the sphere of foreign exchange
by such structural changes are not passing but fundamental.
Their effect may not be as dramatic as that of a speculative
attack, or a flight of funds or larger-scale hedging, or a lengthening of leads and lags. The resulting decline in exporting
capacity and the increase in import requirements may produce
gradual and cumulative effects by leading to the progressive
exhaustion of the gold and foreign exchange reserves and to a
progressive increase of external short-term indebtedness. This,
together with the psychological effect of the recurrent weakness of the exchange, is liable to inspire distrust in the currency.
A stage is likely to be reached at which this comes to generate
the direct causes of foreign exchange crises mentioned above.

Such structural changes need not necessarily lead to foreign
exchange crises. If they develop gradually and if the authorities
come to realise in good time what is happening the moribund
or inefficient industries may be replaced or supplemented by
others that would replace the lost export markets and prevent
or offset the effect of the increase in imports.

But in many instances the structural changes are so insidious
that it takes some time before they come to be realised adequately. It is difficult for a country which had held the lead
in the industrial sphere for some two centuries to realise that
in many respects it has lost its lead and in other respects it is
well on the way towards losing it. Apart from relative declines
resulting from the more impressive progress by other industrial
countries and from the industrialisation of agricultural countries, there may be an absolute decline through obsolescence
of equipment, especially of the transport system, through the
demoralisation of industrial labour conditions dealt with in the

next chapter, and through deterioration of management and inventive genius as a result of egalitarian taxation leading to brain drain.

While in 1931 the sterling crisis was largely due to the chronic difficulties of the British export trade resulting from the overvaluation of sterling, today there is no such overvaluation. Since 1967, prices in Britain have been lower than in a number of important industrial countries. That in spite of this it was difficult for Britain to produce an adequate surplus on her balance of payments was largely due to the structural deteriorations which handicap exports. Perhaps a better realisation of the connection between that structural deterioration and the basic weakness of sterling might have gone some way towards the better realisation of the imperative and urgent need for reversing the process.

Structural deterioration in the absolute sense is aggravated by structural deterioration in a relative sense. The failure of Britain to keep pace with some rival industrial nations in the race for increased automation in itself accounts to some extent for the perennial basic weakness of sterling and its vulnerability to more immediate causes making for acute crises. The resistance of trade unions to the adoption of labour-saving equipment, and their insistence on conditions that deprive their employers of most of the benefits derived from the adoption of such equipment, is a major obstacle to a lasting solution of the problem of combining expansion of output with stability of sterling. Other countries with a more enlightened and less anti-social trade union movement are making better progress and Britain is left behind.

CHAPTER SIXTEEN

NATIONAL DEMORALISATION

By far the gravest danger to the stability of an exchange lies in a national demoralisation. So long as a nation's morale is right its Government is able to cope with any difficulties, and a solution of its foreign exchange crisis can be found in a relatively short time. The Government can rely on the nation's willingness to accept the necessary hardships and is in a position to take swift and effective action. Such a display of firmness and determination in face of adversity is bound to impress the foreign exchange market favourably, so that the material effects of the defensive measures become reinforced by its psychological effects.

But if such is the prevailing spirit of the nation that the Government does not dare to incur unpopularity by applying much-needed drastic remedies then the foreign exchange crisis is bound to drag on and is bound to become aggravated. If the Government itself is so corrupt that it neglects its duty because it wants to avoid losing votes by adopting unpopular measures, it is an indication of national demoralisation, because every nation has the Government it deserves.

National demoralisation is liable to arise through two diametrically opposite causes — complacency and defeatism. A prolonged period of prosperity is liable to breed complacency. All sectional interests come to assume that prosperity will go on forever, and they all endeavour to secure for themselves the maximum benefit, in total disregard to the interests of other sectors or of the community as a whole. In the apparent absence of any menace to national prosperity or stability, they do not feel any need for restraining their desire to be guided entirely by their self-interest. Such an attitude, once established, is apt to survive the era of prosperity. It suits the sectional interests to ignore, or pretend to ignore, the gathering clouds of a foreign exchange crisis and to continue to behave as if the nation had concluded a contract with providence for the maintenance of perpetual prosperity.

At the opposite extreme, some major disaster such as a war or a civil war, or a prolonged period of political or economic instability, is liable to breed defeatism. Sectional interests adopt the attitude that it would be useless to try to resist the tide of adversity by means of isolated acts of sacrifice, since any unselfishness on the part of their sector would be wasted in face of the assumed unrestrained selfishness of other sectors.

In the short run complacency is the smaller of the two evils from the point of view of their effects on foreign exchanges. Indeed it may even help in maintaining the exchange because it generates within the nation an unwarranted degree of confidence in the stability of the national currency. But precisely because of this, it conveys the impression that there is no need for drastic measures to save the exchange. In the long run, therefore, complacency is a mortal menace to exchange. During the first World War the extent of the depreciation of the exchanges of the belligerent countries — with the exception of Russia — was kept down, in some instances by official pegging of the rates, but in other instances by the prevailing confidence in the ultimate return to pre-war rates. Had it not been for this complacency, bigger efforts might have been made, at any rate in some countries, to resist the process of deterioration. Even after the war, amidst runaway inflation and rapidly depreciating exchanges, complacency in respect of the likelihood of an ultimate return to the old parities kept down the pace of the depreciation until the hopelessness of the situation came to be realised. Then the pendulum swung in the opposite direction and complacency gave way to defeatism.

In the case of Germany demoralisation came to assume extreme dimensions by the beginning of the 'twenties. Hopes for maintaining the mark were abandoned and there was no serious attempt to check its avalanche-like depreciation. The same thing happened, though to a less extreme degree, in other

Central and Eastern European countries. Amidst the demoralisation of these nations their Governments were unable to resort to drastic remedies until they were able to do so under compulsion, as part of international economic reconstruction schemes. It is now generally recognised that the financial discipline forced on these Governments had helped their exchanges much more than the loans for the sake of which they were willing to submit to the discipline.

Long after these countries stabilised their exchanges the currencies of countries whose crises had not been considered to be sufficiently grave to justify such international salvage action continued to suffer through national demoralisation. For instance, France suffered a series of foreign exchange crises between 1919 and 1926, because her Governments deemed it impossible to impose on the nation the degree of hardships that would have been necessary in order to stabilise the franc. Inflation had been both cause and effect of the temporary deterioration of the national character. It played havoc with the traditional thrift and conservatism of the French people, as it undermined the traditional self-discipline of the German people.

After the short-lived stability of exchanges in the late 'twenties and the opening year of the 'thirties, most currencies relapsed once more into chaos, owing to the abandonment of the discipline forced on the countries concerned by the need to maintain a stable currency. Because of the prolonged depression it had become a virtue both for individuals and for their Governments to spend as much as possible. The Governments outdid each other in their efforts to secure short-lived advantages from depreciating their exchanges. Following on their prolonged supreme effort to maintain stability, even the countries of the Gold Bloc submitted to growing pressure on their exchanges. In the case of France and Belgium the abandonment of stability was followed by another spell of national demoralisation amidst which devaluations and changes of unstable Governments followed each other in close succession.

The second World War witnessed the imposition of the

highest degree of almost universal exchange control that has ever been in operation. The control survived the war and was only dismantled very gradually. But in many countries it did not prevent the development of a succession of foreign exchange crises. Extreme inflation in China, Hungary and Greece played havoc with the exchanges. Even countries such as France and Italy relapsed to the conditions that had existed during the 'twenties, although the depreciations were more systematically regulated most of the time. In Britain exchange control did not prevent in 1949 a foreign exchange crisis that forced the Government to devalue sterling. It was devalued again in 1967 and the franc followed in 1969.

After the restoration of a high degree of freedom in foreign exchange markets during the 'fifties foreign exchange crises continued to occur at frequent intervals. In France, before the advent of General de Gaulle, it was largely the result of demoralisation due to political instability, though external Government expenditure, too, played a part in it.

In the U.S., after a long period of successful maintenance of economic stability through stop-go, the insatiable appetite for domestic growth and also for expansion of American investment abroad, together with heavy military expenditure abroad and the cost of economic and military aid to foreign Governments, resulted in perennial pressure on the dollar which was met out of the gold reserve. While originally there was an adequate export surplus, in the late 'fifties the gradual decline of the gold reserve and the simultaneous increase in external short-term indebtedness had weakened the dollar's formerly impregnable technical strength. Instead of resorting to timely measures to remedy this state of affairs, the U.S. authorities, with the full approval of the American public, watched the rapid deterioration of the position without taking action that would have maintained the strength of the dollar at the cost of moderating the pace of the non-stop expansion.

American demoralisation assumed the form of complacency in face of the warning signals of declining gold reserves and increasing foreign deposits. Wishful-thinking American politicians, economists and the public succeeded in persuading themselves that they had solved the mystery of combining progress with stability. They felt they no longer needed to apply stop-go in order to prevent a deterioration of their balance of payments; they just allowed their balance of payments to continue to deteriorate and paid the perennial deficits out of their gold reserves.

This attitude recalls the 'gospel of the Brothers Barnabas' in Shaw's *Back to Methuselah*, under whose creed longevity was hoped to be achieved by the simple device of firmly believing in its feasibility. Likewise the U.S. administrations in the late 'fifties and in the early and middle 'sixties believed that by believing in non-stop growth and everlasting prosperity it could be made into reality. They actually reduced taxation in the middle of a boom in 1965 when the situation called for deflationary measures. They encouraged, right until 1965, the outflow of American capital, and did not discourage it effectively even after that year in which long-overdue measures to moderate and reverse the outflow came to be adopted.

There was an orgy of wasteful spending within the country, symbolised by the Americans' desire to have a motor-car for each member of the family, to change it for a new model every year, and to increase the size of the cars to absurdly inconvenient proportions. It may be said that, while Britain jeopardised the stability of sterling for the sake of the welfare state and overfull-employment, the United States allowed the reserves defending the dollar to weaken for the sake of the ideal of a new model of automobile each year.

The worst of it is that the American anti-stop-go attitude came to inspire a similar policy in Britain in the middle 'sixties, even though the technical defences of sterling were incomparably weaker than those of the dollar. While the U.S. could afford to lose gold year after year, in Britain the idea of non-stop prosperity led to a spectacular increase of the adverse trade balance in 1964 and to an increase of the international short-term indebtedness in subsequent years.

E

Demoralisation in Britain that has been responsible for the chronic sickness of the pound was largely the result of the unwillingness of post-war Governments to try to restore discipline in British industry. From the adoption of the Beveridge Plan onward, concession after concession was made to the working classes without requiring them to reciprocate in the form of putting in an honest day's work for their increased pay.

Britain, having won the war at a tremendous cost, lost the peace at the Press conference when the Beveridge Plan was announced. I can still hear Lord Beveridge's words with which he presented his plan of social security as something absolutely inevitable. 'To those who ask me, Can we afford to have it ?, my answer is, Can we afford not to have it ?' The costly social benefits to be introduced under the plan were thus presented to the beneficiaries as their birthright to which they are absolutely entitled regardless of whether they contribute towards earning the costs running into many thousands of millions of pounds.

Of course the correct way of presenting the plan would have been : 'We don't know whether we can afford to have it. This is in the way of being an experiment, whether it succeeds depends on you and *you* and YOU! If you work hard enough to enable the community to earn the extra costs we can afford it. If not, we may have to scale it down and may even have to repeal it.'

Every subsequent concession to the working classes was granted in the same spirit, unconditionally; though the Government of the day paid occasional lip service to the need for working hard, nobody took it too seriously, not even the Government concerned. The Government and the community had come to be looked upon by the working classes as Santa Claus who gives away everything without expecting anything in return. Even those few trade union leaders who had realised the mistake could do nothing about the resulting demoralisation. They could not possibly have obtained support for any attempt to induce their members voluntarily to reciprocate Santa Claus's free gifts.

As a result the British working classes came to take it for

granted that they have only rights and no duties towards the community. They claimed it to be their basic birthright to secure the maximum benefit out of the community while reducing to a minimum their contribution towards the wealth of their community. This attitude is not confined to Britain, but it prevails in Britain to such an extent that it has come to be known as 'the English disease' throughout the world. The main manifestations of that 'disease' may be summarised as follows :

(1) The scarcity of labour was exploited by the trade unions to the utmost for securing the maximum benefits, without any effort to earn and deserve such additional benefits.

(2) Rounds of unearned wage increases were enforced once or twice a year in the absence of corresponding increases in productivity, and regardless of whether profits were rising or falling.

(3) At the same time reductions in the working week were enforced, mainly in order to be able to earn more overtime pay at increased rates.

(4) For the sake of earning more overtime pay the output per man-hour was kept down deliberately.

(5) Members of trade unions systematically dishonoured agreements freely negotiated by their elected representatives, as soon as there was a chance for extorting additional benefits through unofficial strikes, bans on overtime, go-slow, etc.

(6) Such unofficial strikes, which were often embarked upon on the flimsiest of excuses, very often ended in being made official. In any case even unofficial strikers could rely on being protected by the whole labour movement against the consequences of their action.

(7) In the absence of adequate industrial discipline the quality of manufactures deteriorated. Attempts to prevent this were liable to result in unofficial strikes.

(8) Delivery dates in contracts became utterly undependable. Exporters, in order to avoid having to pay high penalties for default on delivering in accordance with

contract, had to quote very long delivery dates, thereby losing many contracts.

(9) Absenteeism increased, because many employees could afford the luxury of taking days off for watching their favourite sports events, or just for taking it easy.

(10) Under a wide variety of restrictive practices a number of totally idle had to be kept on the payroll, or the work was spread over an unnecessarily large number of semi-idle hands.

The above list is by no means complete. The subject is discussed in greater detail in my book *Decline and Fall?* But the above examples of the manifestations of the 'English disease' should suffice to show the way deterioration of the national character has created conditions in which sterling came to be exposed to pressure leading to a succession of crises.

While other countries have their labour problems and there have been indications of a spreading of the 'English disease' in Germany and other countries, in no other major industrial country are working classes nearly so anti-social as in Britain. They seek to satisfy their legitimate claim to participate in increased prosperity not through assisting the community to increase the output but through securing unearned wage increases to the detriment of managements, shareholders, consumers and fellow-workers in other trade unions. So long as such spirit prevails there can be very little done to strengthen sterling against chronic crises, and any recoveries achieved through deflationary measures are bound to be purely temporary.

Even if the Government's efforts to induce unions to put their house in order should prove to be successful, the years of the 'sixties would long be remembered as the years of the locusts. The contrast with Italy, Germany, Japan and other countries, where the early adoption of drastic measures produced the desired effects in a matter of months, gives an idea of the extent to which the British nation, formerly a model of sound finance based on the national character, has deteriorated.

PART THREE

REMEDIES

CHAPTER SEVENTEEN

DRAWING ON RESERVES

HAVING examined the main causes, direct and indirect, of
foreign exchange crises, our next step is to examine the ways
in which such crises are met. In many instances the Governments concerned chose to take the line of least resistance, by
simply using up their reserves or by selling for forward delivery
foreign exchanges they did not possess, or by borrowing abroad,
or by abandoning the defence of their parities. In other instances the Governments put up a defence in the form of deflation, or incomes policy, or export drives or exchange control.

There are innumerable devices that can be applied in face
of a foreign exchange crisis, but here we are only concerned
with the major policies :

(1) Letting reserves run down.
(2) Supplementing depleted reserves by borrowing.
(3) Trying to strengthen the exchange by export drives.
(4) Applying 'stop-go'.
(5) Applying exchange control or import control.
(6) Applying an incomes policy.
(7) Devaluing the currency.
(8) Allowing exchange rates to find their level.
(9) Raising the price of gold.
(10) Joining the Common Market.
(11) Achieving national regeneration.

The present chapter deals with one of the favourite ways of
taking the line of least resistance by drawing on the reserves
to meet a selling pressure on the exchange. Faced with a foreign exchange crisis, the policy applied by most Governments
is, to begin with at any rate, to allow its reserves to decline.
This is justified and necessary until it becomes evident that the
pressure on the exchange is not just a passing tendency which

could and should be met out of reserves, provided that it could be done without depleting them unduly. It would not be reasonable to expect a Government to resort to defensive measures which are bound to be unpopular, merely for the sake of meeting a perfectly normal routine seasonal demand for foreign exchanges. It would be like killing a mosquito with a sledgehammer.

Although some monetary authorities are endowed with an over-developed gold-hoarding instinct and are traditionally inclined to resist even minor declines of their reserves, most Central Banks and Treasuries duly realise that reserves exist for the purpose of being used. It is only when there appears to be a possibility that the decline of the reserves is likely to be substantial that they begin to feel the need for taking action.

There are very few countries which have sufficiently large reserves to be able to weather a major crisis simply by allowing their reserves to run down until the trend has changed. The United States is, or was until recently, among the fortunate few. Most other countries have a more or less narrow margin beyond the amount which they feel they must preserve. Even if it is no major disaster if the reserves should decline temporarily below that limit, should the decline continue and if there seems to be a possibility that real danger level might be reached, steps are taken in order to call a halt to the decline.

The whereabouts of the danger level depends among other factors on the country's foreign trade. A country with a small volume of foreign trade does not require a large reserve, because the fluctuations of its trade balance are likely to be smaller than those of the trade balance of a country with a large volume of foreign trade. A country with a reserve currency or with a large turnover in international financial transactions needs a larger reserve than a country whose currency is of limited international significance. A country whose population is inclined to engage in flights of capital needs a larger reserve than a country the bulk of whose population is not in the habit of being frightened into transferring their money abroad. **Anyhow, all monetary authorities have presumably a figure in** mind, even if they are inclined to reconsider it from time to time. Any decline, or threat to decline, below that figure is apt to induce them to resort to various measures to ensure that the selling pressure on their exchange is mitigated. They cease to depend solely on their reserves to see them through the crisis.

Official policies regarding the extent to which pressure should be met with the aid of the reserves vary. During the 19th century and right to the first World War the leading continental countries — especially France and Germany — aimed at maintaining a large reserve in excess of their immediate needs, in part presumably for the sake of being able to meet war requirements. Britain, on the other hand, in spite of her large international trade and other international financial commitments, never aimed at maintaining a large gold reserve. Between the wars sterling was maintained precariously between 1925 and 1931 on an inadequate gold reserve. In more recent years, too, the British reserve was lower than that of other leading countries especially if we make allowances for sterling's role as a reserve currency.

During 1964, when Britain was only just recovering from a recession, the Chancellor of the Exchequer, Mr Maudling, was reluctant to resort to new deflationary measures for the sake of correcting the increasingly adverse trade balance. He declared himself in favour of the principle that in given circumstances deficits could and should be met by allowing the reserve to run down. The question is, was he justified in assuming that the deficit was purely temporary and that he was entitled, therefore, to face it without a major squeeze or other defensive measures? We shall never know, because the election of October 1964 brought to power a Socialist Government under which the deficit, while fluctuating from year to year, continued. What would have happened to sterling if a Conservative Government had been returned remains one of the innumerable 'ifs' of history over which politicians and politically minded economists will argue till the end of time.

E 2

CHAPTER EIGHTEEN

BORROWING ABROAD

ONE of the easy ways in which inadequate reserves are supplemented in order to be able to resist a persistent pressure on the exchange is to borrow abroad. That is to say, it is easy if the country whose exchange is under pressure is deemed creditworthy, or if a devaluation of its currency is considered to endanger the stability of the lending countries' currencies. Such borrowing, which may assume various forms, does not constitute a solution. Sooner or later the borrower will have to repay the amount borrowed, and in the case of short-term borrowing that moment arrives sooner rather than later — unless, of course, the creditors deem it expedient to renew their loans over and over again. The borrower wants to defer repayment until its foreign exchange crisis has come to an end. Repayment in the real sense of the term is then made — indeed it can only be made — out of balance of payments surpluses. Of course official short-term liabilities can be consolidated into long-term liabilities. They can also be repaid by attracting private balances. But neither of these methods constitutes a repayment in the real sense.

The following are the chief existing methods of borrowing undertaken in order to reinforce the reserves:

(1) Using drawing rights with the IMF.
(2) Obtaining short-term credits from foreign Central Banks and the BIS.
(3) Arranging reciprocal swap facilities with foreign Central Banks.
(4) Attracting foreign private funds by means of high Bank rate.
(5) Attracting foreign private funds by means of forward exchange tactics.

(6) Encouraging the influx of Euro-currency deposits.

(7) Long-term borrowing abroad by the Government.

(8) Encouraging private long-term borrowing abroad.

(9) Encouraging foreign direct investment.

The facilities provided by the IMF have been expanded considerably since the IMF first began its operations. They are very helpful for meeting short and swift crises, but not so helpful if pressure on the exchange persists over years. For repayment is apt to become due before the balance of payments deficit has changed into a surplus. This is what happened in the case of British drawings on the IMF. Repayments due from 1967 presented a difficult problem, for in the course of the years further short-term liabilities were created. They had to be renewed or consolidated.

Although reciprocal swap facilities are standing arrangements their actual use is usually subject to the approval of the Central Bank whose currency is to be sold in support of the exchange under pressure. It may occur that both currencies come under pressure, in which case the arrangement is useless. Nor can it be used, as a rule, to counteract pressure from a third currency. The swap arrangement between the Bank of England and the Netherlands Bank, for instance, can be used by the former to offset a selling pressure on sterling from Amsterdam or by the latter to offset a selling pressure on the guilder from London. But neither Central Bank finds it useful for offsetting the selling pressure on both of their currencies simultaneously from Paris.

Central Bank credits of a more conventional kind are usually for limited brief periods and are renewable every 3 months or 6 months. So are, for that matter, reciprocal swap facilities. They are useful to meet an immediate attack if there is reason to hope that it would become reversed within that brief period. Non-renewal of the credits by some of the major participants might greatly aggravate the crisis. Speculation on the mere possibility of non-renewal has been repeatedly the cause of acute attacks on sterling in 1965 and 1966.

The conventional way of reinforcing reserves is by means of

an increase of the Bank rate. But the use of the Bank rate during the past by the Bank of England was not a matter of borrowing, it was mainly enforcing the repayment of outstanding claims by making them too costly for the debtor. This was during the period when world trade was largely financed with the aid of sterling credits, and the reduction of the outstanding amount of sterling bills through repayments on maturity or through the rediscounting of bills abroad constituted a highly efficient way of reinforcing the British gold reserve.

Today the sterling bill plays a secondary part in international financing, and the extent to which high Bank rate can reinforce British reserves is limited. For one thing, when sterling is under a cloud debtors in sterling prefer to maintain their debts in the hope of repayment in devalued sterling. Nor does a high Bank rate by itself attract foreign money unless there is a net profit on inward arbitrage after allowing for the cost of forward covering. The main object of high interest rates in existing circumstances is not borrowing but improving the balance of payments by means of deflating the overheated economy.

In addition to the conventional method of stimulating private borrowing, the authorities have developed the use of more modern devices. Foremost among them is the pursuit of forward exchange tactics with an object of assisting inward arbitrage. If, as a result of official buying of the local currency for forward delivery, its forward rates appreciate above their interest parities it becomes profitable for arbitrageurs to secure the temporary use of foreign currencies by means of swap transactions and invest these currencies into short-term loans, deposits or securities. This was what was happening on a very large scale during 1964–67 in respect of forward sterling. The resulting influx of foreign funds mitigated the decline of the reserve and also the extent to which Central Bank credits had to be drawn upon. What it really amounted to was that import surpluses were paid for largely with the aid of foreign currencies obtained through inward arbitrage stimulated artificially by means of official support to forward sterling. More will be said about this in Chapter 22.

To a very large degree such inward arbitrage takes place between sterling and Euro-currencies. But there are other means by which it is possible for the monetary authorities to increase their reserves, or prevent the decline of their reserves, by encouraging the swapping of Euro-currencies into the national currency. Several monetary authorities — especially those of Germany, Italy and Japan — have brought the technique of managing movements in and out of Euro-currencies to a fine art. They themselves may offer local banks swap arrangements on terms which largely determine whether funds move into or out of the national currency. Or they adjust reserve requirements on such funds according to whether they want funds to flow into or out of the country.

Yet another method of supplementing the reserves is by means of issuing foreign loans for Governments or official institutions, or encouraging long-term issues by private firms in foreign markets. The development of the Euro-bond market has greatly assisted in the increased use of that device, as it has enabled borrowing countries to issue loans outside the U.S. and outside the few other countries which had limited surpluses available for lending abroad. A high proportion of subscribers consists of holders of refugee funds. Borrowing in the broader sense of the term may assume the form of placing equity capital in foreign countries, or foreign direct investment in the country concerned. The same effect is achieved by encouraging disinvestment by holders of foreign securities or of direct investments abroad.

Beyond doubt, such long-term transactions compare favourably with short-term borrowing from the point of view of ensuring the borrowing country the possession of the additional reserve over long periods. On the other hand, generally speaking, the interest or dividend payments on such long-term borrowing are usually heavier than the cost of short-term credits for corresponding amounts. But the main disadvantage of this method is that its application obviates the necessity for urgent and drastic action to bring the foreign exchange crisis to an end with the aid of the sacrifices and exertions of the country concerned. It is taking the line of least resistance to solve the immediate problem by assuming the burden of a long-term debt, or selling out valuable foreign assets, or selling out even more valuable domestic industrial assets to foreign buyers.

The main criticism of the policy aiming at increasing or maintaining reserves by means of attracting private short-term funds is that it makes the exchange even more vulnerable. We saw in Chapter 2 that withdrawals of foreign funds are apt to initiate or aggravate foreign exchange crises. The need for retaining foreign balances is apt to force the authorities to maintain the Bank rate at a higher level than is warranted by the state of the domestic economy. This disadvantage can be mitigated, if not eliminated altogether, by a sensible use of forward exchange policy. The authorities can regulate the swap rate in a way as to regulate the inflow and outflow of foreign balances in accordance with the requirements of their monetary policy. That refined device should only be used, however, in moderation, to tide over temporary difficulties. It should not be used as the principal device of foreign exchange policy, to take the place of regulating the basic trend of the economy. This controversial question will be dealt with in greater detail in Chapter 22.

The establishment of the IMF and the gradual increase of the amount of drawing rights available for its member Governments, culminating in the creation of SDRs, together with the arrangement of Central Bank credits and reciprocal drawing rights, has institutionalised the use of foreign credits as a means for coping with foreign exchange crises. It is hardly justified to class these devices among the remedies of foreign exchange crises. Indeed, by making it too easy to receive external support, they have made it too tempting for Governments to refrain from applying effective remedies.

CHAPTER NINETEEN

EXPORT DRIVES

A FORMULA popular in certain politically minded circles is that Britain's balance of payments difficulties were due to the alleged unwillingness of British business firms to devote sufficient effort to developing their foreign markets. They were accused of preferring the line of least resistance by selling their goods in the domestic market rather than incurring trouble, expense and risk by embarking on export drives on an adequate scale. No doubt it would be possible to produce enough evidence to show that the exporting efforts of many firms and even of entire industries leave much to be desired and could be stepped up considerably. But given the high and rising costs of British manufactures during the 'fifties and the 'sixties because of high wages received for inadequate effort, and the long and undependable delivery dates due to trade-union practices and malpractices, it seems little short of a miracle that British firms had been able to increase their exports in spite of having been handicapped by the attitude of their employees and of the Government.

In so far as most of the criticism of the exporting effort comes from trade unionists and Socialists, the answer is that the remedy lay very largely in their own hands. By moderating their demand for unearned wages and, even more, by trying to give a fair day's work for their pay, industrial workers could have made the prices of British exports much more competitive and delivery dates more acceptable and reliable than they were in recent years. In so far as the criticism came from Government spokesmen — as it often did — the answer is again that the remedy lay largely in the critics' hands. By abstaining from pursuing policies which inflated consumer demand, the Government could have forced industries to pay more attention to their overseas markets. But then it is easier to blame others rather than to do the right thing.

In fairness it must be admitted that the Government did adopt right policies at times, but not until after its realisation of the failure of increasing exports by means of exhortation aiming at persuading business firms to export even if it is easier and more profitable to sell at home.

In the course of its attempt at 'government by exhortation' during 1964–69, the Labour Government did in fact endeavour to induce British firms to concentrate more effort on their export trade. In addition to appeals to their public spirit, executives of firms which proved themselves successful in expanding their overseas markets were promised — though perhaps not in so many words — places in the honours lists. There were some fiscal concessions — though not sufficient to make a real difference — and firms engaged in export trade enjoyed privileged treatment by their banks amidst the credit squeeze. Above all, the medium- and long-term credit facilities of the Export Credit Guarantees department were improved and increased.

Exhortations of business firms to induce them to concentrate on exports failed of course to produce miracles. But it was incomparably more effective than the exhortations to workers to work harder in the public interest. Businessmen were anxious not to antagonise the Socialist Government for fear of unspecified reprisals. Indeed the influence of the Government on industrial firms and their trade associations was a multiple of such influence as they were able to exert on workers or on their trade unions. So in many instances business firms were induced to forgo larger and easier profits on domestic sales. I have not come across any recorded instances of sacrifices on the part of workers for the sake of helping the export drive in order to save the pound.

Of all the methods that stimulate exports, that of increasing long-term credit facilities was the most futile. Because of the acute sterling crisis, foreign exchange was needed, not in ten or fifteen years' time but immediately. The granting of long-term credit facilities simply increased current export for statistical purposes. At the same time, however, it lengthened the lags. Moreover, it reduced the extent to which industries were able or willing to export for immediate payment or against the conventional short-term credits. Firms which, thanks to the official facilities at their disposal, were able to offer long-term credits were able to obtain more favourable prices than those insisting on short credits. Consequently they preferred to sell on a long-term credit basis instead of trying to increase their exports by cutting their costs and their prices, or by improving the quality of their goods.

This brings us to the major objection to the artificial ways of stimulating exports at a time when industries have little or no unused capacity. During a period of large-scale unemployment export drives are useful because they can reduce the import surplus or increase the export surplus. If, however, inflated domestic purchasing power keeps domestic demand at a high level, and overfull-employment makes it difficult to increase total output materially, any increase of exports merely tends to entail a corresponding increase of imports.

To illustrate this point let us take an example based on experience. Thanks to long-term credit facilities placed at their disposal, British shipyards were able to sell additional ships to Communist countries and to other foreign countries. Since, however, the additional orders made their delivery dates even longer and even less dependable, British shipping companies and oil companies had to order their ships and their tankers abroad. This meant that since the British ships were sold on a long-term credit basis but foreign ships were bought on a cash basis, there was a net immediate loss to the balance of payments. And there is at least a possibility that some of the ships sold on long-term credit might never be paid for at all.

Of course conditions concerning the export of consumer goods on a credit basis are different. But even in this respect the additional wages paid out as a result of a successful export drive create additional consumer demand, part of which

increases imports. It also aggravates the scarcity of labour
making it more difficult for exporters to deliver their goods in
time.

The ease with which industrial firms were able to unload
their output in the inflated domestic market compared favourably with the difficulties that exporters not benefiting by
Government-guaranteed long-term credit facilities were bound
to encounter in foreign markets. Apart from having to compete
with foreign firms, they had to overcome sundry obstacles
placed by foreign Governments in the way of imports. Having
spent a great deal to establish themselves in a foreign market,
they were exposed to the loss of that investment through some
change in Government regulations in the importing countries
or through some successful drive to buy local products in
preference to importing foreign goods. It is no wonder that
in spite of all exhortations, inducement and pressure, most
firms preferred to sell at home so long as the domestic market
had an increasing absorbing capacity.

The only way in which firms can be effectively induced to
step up their export drives is through cutting down their domestic markets by means of reducing purchasing power. This
was done in 1968 through higher taxation and import deposits.

It may be arguable that a reduction of the domestic market
tends to increase the cost of production per unit, by reducing
the benefit derived from producing on a larger scale. But a
fall in sales at home could be partly offset by the increase in
sales abroad, in which case the cost per unit would not be
affected so much. Moreover, the need for competing with
more efficient foreign rivals instead of working for the home
market which is to some extent sheltered from foreign rivals
might induce many industrial firms to make a supreme effort
to become more efficient. This might go some way towards
offsetting the increase of their cost per unit resulting from the
decline of their output.

Above all, in so far as production for export takes the place
of production for the domestic market instead of being additional to it, the overload on the economy would not increase

and trade unions are not provided with additional opportunities for stepping up their demands. Indeed, since manufacturers have to compete with foreign rivals they have to resist excessive wage demands, instead of conceding them after a mere token resistance on the safe assumption that wages paid by other British firms also go up. The effect of stiffening resistance on the trend of wages, prices and costs would benefit the exchange. This is in contrast to export drives unaccompanied by contraction of the domestic market.

Industrial firms might even be able to argue successfully with trade unions that the decline in domestic demand threatens to cause redundancy which could only be avoided if an effort is made to produce more efficiently and at a lower cost for more difficult foreign markets. Of course trade unions would insist on their part that increased efficiency should also apply to managements, which would be all to the good. By insisting that in return for an extra effort on the part of their members to help the export drive, managements, too, must make a supreme effort, trade unions would play a constructive role.

Experience in Britain has conclusively proved that, while official exhortations might induce managements to some extent to step up their export drives, they are worse than useless for inducing workers to make an extra effort, or indeed to abstain from strikes that are liable to damage exports. Such exhortations only make them even more conscious of their nuisance value and induce them to step up their excessive wage demands, on the assumption that their firms and the country could not afford a strike.

The improvement of the trade balance during the second half of 1969 did not affect the validity of the above arguments. The increase in exports was largely due to the expansion of world trade. For instance, such was the demand for ships that even British shipyards with their higher costs and longer delivery dates were bound to benefit by it.

CHAPTER TWENTY

STOP-GO

THROUGHOUT most of the post-war period the stability of the principal exchanges was defended largely with the aid of the policy of 'stop-go' — that is, the application of various measures to relieve the overload of the economy at the time of foreign exchange crises and the removal of the measures and encouragement of expansion in between such crises. This policy is largely based on Keynesian principles. Although pre-Keynesian counter-cyclical monetary devices such as Bank rate changes and the regulation of the volume of credit also played a very important part, they were supplemented by Budgetary policies, measures aimed at reductions and increases of capital spending, and by selective measures aimed at influencing consumption through influencing the volume of hire-purchase credits.

In the 'forties and the 'fifties such measures were usually applied before inflationary expansion got out of control. Indeed the major cyclic crises of the pre-war type came to be replaced by minor recessions and recoveries brought about in more frequent intervals. They were incomparably milder than the pre-war crises, and the extent of unemployment that accompanied them was much more moderate.

As a general rule — especially as far as Britain was concerned — the 'stop' was seldom applied for purely domestic reasons. The authorities abstained from interfering with the almost continuous process of creeping inflation that accompanied their expansionary policies resulting in full and overfull employment so long as it confined its effect to an erosion of the domestic purchasing power of the currency. They did not resort to 'stop' until inflation came to affect the exchange and the reserves. And as soon as the immediate danger to the reserves abated they hastened to revert to 'go'.

Though far from being an ideal system, the policy of 'stop-go' saved the post-war world from slumps and from major recessions. Although it slowed down the overall pace of growth, that pace became less uneven and was not interrupted by major setbacks. Although technological progress became accelerated considerably, it was not accompanied by mass unemployment, not even in the U.S. where automation was going ahead with leaps and bounds during the 'fifties and 'sixties. It was thanks to 'stop-go' that those who had predicted that unemployment comparable with that of the 'thirties would develop as a result of automation have proved to have been false prophets.

Notwithstanding its obvious advantages, the defence against foreign exchange crises on the 'one stitch in time saves nine' principle became increasingly unpopular in the Anglo-Saxon world. 'Stop-go' became a term of abuse in political controversies. Outcries aroused by mild recessions caused by it from time to time were in no way inferior to the bursts of indignation caused by major slumps of past periods. Indeed since in the past business cycles had been looked upon as acts of God while post-war 'stops' were obviously man-made, critics of 'stop-go' have exhausted their vocabulary of invective in their denunciation of the new policy, so that they are in danger of being unable to do justice to a real slump should they ever find themselves confronted with one.

The report produced by the Plowden Committee on that subject is largely responsible for the initiation of the anti-'stop-go' crusade. It denounced that policy in no uncertain terms, though largely on the ridiculously flimsy ground that it is frustrating for Government officials if their carefully elaborated plans are interfered with by 'stop-go' measures. The Committee's attitude implied that in their opinion whenever the Government finds itself confronted with the necessity of adopting harsh measures in order to defend sterling it should confine those measures to the private sector of the economy. The

public sector must be exempted from any 'stop' measures and
the original plans adopted in totally different circumstances
should be carried through unaltered, regardless of the crying
need for damping down the overheated economy.

The answer which that silly contention deserves is that if
the public interest calls for cuts in previously approved plans
of Government spending the frustrating effect of such cuts on
officials responsible for the elaboration of the plans should be
mitigated by an appropriate psycho-analytical treatment at
public expense. Even in these days of increased Harley Street
fees this would cost a great deal less in the long run than the
suggested alternative of proceeding with the original plans
regardless of the change in the situation, merely for the sake
of sparing the officials the minor inconvenience of feeling
frustrated. It did not even occur to the authors of the Plowden
Report that businessmen, too, are in the habit of planning
ahead their capital expenditure, and that they too feel frustrated
if their plans are upset by changes in Government policies.

The adoption of dear money, credit squeeze and other devices aimed at relieving the overload on the economy is not
sufficiently effective unless it goes far enough to bring about
a change in the attitude of trade unions. It is not so much the
extent to which these measures reduce employment that matters
as the response of the trade unions to such reductions. Mitigation of pressure for higher wages through reducing overfull-
employment tends to moderate both cost inflation and demand
inflation. There will be larger exportable surpluses available
at lower prices. The sooner that end is attained the sooner it
becomes safe, from the point of view of the exchange, to end
the 'stop' and resume the 'go'.

Of course high interest rates assist the exchange that is subject to selling pressure also through their direct effect on the
international movement of funds. Moreover, they usually
inspire confidence, though not necessarily so. If the crisis is
too deep-rooted even an 8 per cent Bank rate does not provide
the answer to it, unless it is accompanied by other defensive
measures sufficiently drastic to impress the market with the

Government's determination to defend the existing exchange parities even at the cost of unpopular measures. The British experience of 1965, when a prolonged high Bank rate, so far from damping down the domestic economy, failed even to prevent an accentuation of the evil of overfull-employment, proves once and for all that drastic additional 'stop' measures are essential in order to make the high Bank rate effective.

The proof of the pudding is in its eating. For nearly two decades 'stop-go' enabled the financially advanced countries to enjoy an almost uninterrupted growth at a relatively high rate. In the absence of 'stops' such a continuous expansion would have greatly accelerated the pace of creeping inflation and would have generated a speculative boom similar to that of the late 'twenties. In due course the world would have experienced a major setback with incalculable economic, financial, social and political consequences.

From this point of view the discipline forced on Governments by foreign exchange crises is a blessing in disguise. Otherwise, in the absence of an acute threat of exchange depreciation and depletion of reserves, they might not be willing to defy public opinion by resorting to unpopular measures and domestic inflationary boom would be allowed to proceed unhampered. To the extent to which the 'gnomes' are responsible for foreign exchange crises the world owes them a debt of gratitude.

It was largely owing to the inability of the British Labour Government to solve the sterling crisis between 1964 and 1969 that 'stop' measures have come to be considered ineffective. The answer is that they were ineffective because the Government did not mean them to be really effective so long as it hoped to be able to solve the crisis painlessly. While paying lip-service to deflation the Government took good care for five years to avoid any measure that would have greatly reduced employment. Until the end of 1965 the excess of vacancies over the number of unemployed actually increased; the Government actually claimed credit for having succeeded in aggravating the scarcity of labour. Not until July 1966 did it come to realise that it is not to the best interests of the country to aim at overfull-employment.

There can be little doubt that had the Labour Government resorted to effective 'stop' measures in 1964 it would have been in a position to revert to 'go' policies within a year or so. Those means, resorted to in good time, would not have had to be nearly so drastic as the sum total of the successive batches of long-delayed measures adopted eventually. But the Government combined inadequate deflationary measures with distinctly inflationary policies. In a minor way, it did practise a measure of 'stop-go' with its inadequate defensive policies, mitigating the squeeze each time the sterling crisis appeared to abate under the immediate impact of the latest instalment of these measures, or even as a result of a renewal of foreign Central Bank credits, and reinforcing its measures when their relaxation caused an aggravation of the crisis.

Other countries, especially Germany, Switzerland, Italy and Japan, succeeded in combining expansion with a fair degree of stability by a judicious application of 'stop-go'. On most occasions they did not delay their 'stop' measures unduly but heeded the warning signs of adverse trade balance and declining reserves. It is true, in the middle 'sixties, Italy and Japan allowed their booms to gather momentum, but when the resulting pressure on their exchange made them realise the need for 'stop' measures they did not hesitate to apply them in full force. The result was that in a matter of months the tide turned in their favour and they were in a position to revert to 'go'.

In sharp contrast to this attitude, Britain had been struggling for years with her foreign exchange crisis which threatened the stability of sterling on repeated occasions. Instead of taking effective steps to eliminate the balance of payments deficit it was allowed to continue year after year — though it had its ups and downs — and it was met by increasing the external short-term liabilities. As a result, the measures that had to be adopted eventually had to be made much more drastic than they would have had to be if they had been adopted in 1964. And they had to be maintained for a long period in order to emerge from the crisis and to repay the indebtedness incurred in defence of sterling. This is the price a nation has to pay for allowing its leaders to forswear 'stop-go' when the defence of the exchange calls for the application of that policy.

The utter futility of the 'stop-go' policy if the 'stop' measures are removed prematurely is illustrated by Britain's experience in 1967. The abatement of the acute pressure on sterling caused by the Israeli war made the British authorities feel justified in relaxing their defensive measures by easing hire-purchase restrictions in August. This irresponsible action inspired a world-wide wave of distrust culminating in the crisis that forced the Government in November to abandon the defences of sterling at its parity of $2.80.

CHAPTER TWENTY-ONE

INCOMES POLICY

Soon after the advent of the Labour Government in 1964 the defence of sterling with the aid of an incomes policy became the Government's declared policy. A declaration of intent was solemnly signed to that effect. The Prices and Incomes Board was set up and an attempt was made to restrain price increases and co-ordinate pay increases by voluntary restraint. This attempt had proved to be a complete unmitigated failure — during 1968 there was a record rise of wages. Under pressure by foreign Central Banks the Government reluctantly decided to obtain moderate statutory powers for the Prices and Incomes Board. In order to make the policy acceptable to the trade unions, the authorities first concentrated their main effort on keeping down prices. During that period the Board spoke with two voices — it was a roaring lion when addressing employers on prices and a cooing dove when addressing employees on wages. The result was that even before statutory powers were obtained prices were kept down to some extent, while wages rose at an accelerated pace. The inflation of consumer purchasing power through the resulting increase in real wages meant that goods which should have been exported were consumed, also that more was imported. It was not a very satisfactory defence of sterling.

It had been widely realised even before the first inadequate experiments were embarked upon in incomes policy that non-stop wage inflation had to be dealt with somehow. But so long as the boom-like conditions created by creeping inflation under overfull-employment continued there was no hope to achieve that end. Scarcity of labour had upset the balance of power between employers and employees, enabling the unions virtually to dictate their terms in total disregard of futile official exhortations to moderate their appetite.

Economists and politicians who had imagined that wage freeze, or even some more moderate form of wage restraint, was a substitute for deflation as the means of restoring the balance of power had been utterly divorced from realities. The experience of 1965–66 conclusively proved that a squeeze was a preliminary condition to the success of a freeze. The fact that a wages policy had been reasonably successful in Holland and in Scandinavia without being reinforced by unduly harsh deflation only goes to show the contrast between the types of trade unionism that exist in Britain and in these countries.

In order to give incomes policy a chance, it became imperative in Britain by the middle 'sixties that the balance of power between employers and employees should be changed through bringing overfull-employment to an end. It became equally necessary to deprive industrial firms of their feeling of absolute certainty that they are able to pass on to the consumer any wage increases they choose to concede. So long as they felt certain to be able to make a profit no matter how much their costs increased they were prepared to concede wage demands, no matter how unreasonable, in order to ensure the continuity of their production and to prevent the loss of their manpower through more favourable terms being obtainable by other firms. To break the vicious wage-price spiral it was absolutely essential to deprive business firms of the certainty of being able to pass on wage increases to the consumer, so as to induce them to risk strikes rather than yield to strike threats. Incomes policy never succeeded in achieving this end.

In practice the Government's policy worked out during 1965 and up to the second half of 1966 in a way as to reduce profit margins without reducing consumer purchasing power or even preventing its further increase. Consequently, while the decline in consumer demand was moderate, there was an appreciable decline in the rate of capital investment. This, rather than the Government's half-hearted efforts to reduce consumer purchasing power, was responsible for the slowing down of the British economy in 1966–67. But later profit margins increased as a result of wage-induced inflation.

It was not until the Government mustered enough courage to obtain statutory powers in order to impose a wage freeze on the trade unions that the incomes policy became partly effective. Even then concessions in respect of some previously agreed wage increases resulted in a slight increase in wages. Small as it was compared with the pace of wage increases in 1965 and the first half of 1966, it was too much, having regard to the fact that there was no increase in productivity.

The wage freeze failed for a long time to inspire in the foreign exchange market the confidence which the Government had expected it to inspire. Together with the Selective Employment Tax and the very drastic measures adopted in July 1966, it was unable to bring about an immediate spectacular turn of the tide in the sterling crisis. During the autumn and winter the Bank of England had to support sterling from time to time, although on balance it was able to buy dollars, especially after the turn of the year. Large-scale short covering only began after the reduction of the Bank rate in January 1967, a gesture which inspired confidence as an indication that the Government is satisfied with sterling's prospects. Yet by that time the wage freeze came to an end and was replaced by wage restraint. Its relaxation in July 1967 led to the devaluation of November 1967.

The degree of speculative anticipation of the effects of the incomes policy was an important factor in the foreign exchange market. Whenever there were indications that the Government meant business and the trade unions were willing to co-operate, at least to some extent, sterling tended to recover. Whenever it was felt, rightly or wrongly, that expectations of results from the new policy had been exaggerated, or whenever there was a distinct setback in its application, sterling became weaker. Speculators and others were watching this situation and arranged their operations accordingly.

Just as the disappointing response of the British economy to the deflationary measures adopted between November 1964

and July 1966 had gone some way towards discrediting deflation as a means for overcoming foreign exchange crises, so
the disappointing response of the foreign exchange market to
income and price restraint in the late sixties has discredited
incomes policy. Right-wing Conservatives, taking advantage
of the inevitable unpopularity of income and price restraint,
embarked on a fanatical *laisser-faire* crusade that would have
done credit to side-whiskered mid-Victorian Liberals.

In reality incomes policy is a very valuable new weapon in
the armoury of Governments, provided that they do not imagine that it could and should replace deflation altogether as
a means for defending the exchanges against crises due to inflation. One of its main advantages consists of enabling the
authorities to achieve the same results with smaller doses of
deflation. To the extent to which trade unions would accept
incomes policy — whether through voluntary action or under
compulsion — they would reduce the extent of unemployment
needed for correcting the imbalance of the economy.

In any event, incomes policy is the only way by which leap-
frogging wage demands could be prevented. Otherwise there
could be no end to the prevailing practice under which lower-
paid unskilled workers enforce wage increases partly for purely
social considerations and partly with the aid of the sheer weight
of their number and in due course semi-skilled and skilled
workers enforce the restoration of the differentials in their
favour. Incomes policy, if successful, could also end wage
blackmail by a small number of key employees who are in a
position to put entire factories out of work. Without an incomes policy it would take a very drastic deflation to prevent
such practices, and such a degree of deflation would expose the
economy to the dangers of a self-aggravating downward spiral.

It is no wonder, therefore, that the foreign exchange market
has come to attach considerable importance to the prospects
of a successful application of incomes policy. The main advantages of its adoption from the point of view of the defence
of the exchange is that it would go some way towards making
various classes of employees realise the relationship of their pay

to that of other classes and to the income-trend of the community as a whole. Such a realisation might go a long way
towards the adoption of an attitude that is less likely to lead
to foreign exchange crises than the present free-for-all. About
this more will be said in Chapter 30.

From the point of view of inducing the workers to accept
wage restraint and incomes policy there may be something to
be said for price restraint and even for restraint on dividends
and profits. But such measures are detrimental to the defence
of the exchange, because, by acting as a disincentive, they
actually handicap progress towards an increase in productivity.
To a large extent price restraint might take the place of
increased efficiency as a means for keeping prices down. From
the point of view of the relative price levels of the country
concerned and of other countries it might make no difference
how prices are kept down, but from the point of view of producing an exportable surplus it would make all the difference.

Moreover, the enforcement of price control and of dividend
restraint greatly discourages the influx of foreign capital and
might even cause a repatriation of formerly imported capital,
to the detriment of the exchange situation.

Because of the inability or unwillingness of trade unions to
take effective steps to prevent unofficial strikes, and even more
their unwillingness to honour contractual obligations, the
Government's efforts to legislate about trade unions gave rise
to hopes about sterling's prospects in the early months of 1969.
It was the abandonment of these efforts that made sterling once
more vulnerable. Fortunately the expansion of world trade,
the rise in American prices and the revaluation of the D. mark
saved sterling from the consequences of that surrender.

CHAPTER TWENTY-TWO

SUPPORTING OF
FORWARD EXCHANGES

THE easiest, and most irresponsible, way of defending the exchange rate of the national currency against adverse pressure is by official intervention in the form of virtually unlimited selling of foreign exchanges for forward delivery. This does not mean that all intervention in the form of forward exchange operations is irresponsible. In given situations it provides a very useful weapon to the monetary authorities, and it can be used for essentially constructive purposes. In my *Dynamic Theory of Forward Exchange* and in my various other writings I explained in detail the circumstances in which the use of that device is legitimate and constructive. But the device lends itself to gross misuse.

The position can best be compared with the way in which paper money, a most valuable institution in the modern monetary system, had been misused by Governments unable to resist the temptation to take the line of least resistance by financing their Budgetary deficit by unlimited issue of such money. From John Law onward the printing press was abused for handing out mandates representing nominal purchasing power created without creating at the same time any real purchasable goods to meet it. Likewise, a Central Bank can sell foreign exchanges it does not possess. It can do so in the hope that by the time the forward contracts mature it would possess them, or that the buyers would anyhow not be in a position to demand delivery without first buying sterling.

By selling forward dollars during the sterling crises of 1964–67 the Bank of England provided the ultimate counterpart for the sales of forward sterling by importers prolonging their leads, by speculators going short in sterling, and by hedgers of every description insuring themselves against losses through a devaluation of sterling. Although the amount of its total commitments remained a closely guarded secret, judging by the figures published by two of the banks which acted for it, the grand total must have exceeded from time to time the total gold and dollar reserve, even if no allowance was made for the foreign Central Bank credits and IMF credits which must be regarded as the first charge on that reserve.

When the Government decided, contrary to its expectations, to devalue sterling, the resulting exchange difference on the outstanding forward contracts was a loss of the Exchange Equalisation Account, and therefore of the British taxpayer. Its amount was estimated at hundreds of millions of pounds. The beneficiaries were almost exclusively non-residents, so that the loss to the Exchequer was also a heavy loss from the point of view of the balance of payments. The risk involved was, therefore, considerable. No matter how much the Government had been determined not to devalue, it was always possible that changes in the situation might force its hands, as indeed they did in 1967.

Because forward facilities were provided at a bargain price, the volume of covering, hedging and speculation must have risen to a multiple of the amount it would have been if supply and demand had been allowed free play in determining the forward margin. In all probability the discount on forward sterling would have risen to a prohibitive figure, at which the majority of hedgers and speculators might not have deemed it worth their while to open or maintain short positions. Leads and lags would not have been lengthened to anything like the extent they were as a result of the abnormally low cost involved.

The main argument in favour of keeping forward discount artificially low is that its widening is liable to increase devaluation fears. That argument may have carried conviction in the inter-war period when selling pressure on an exchange consisted largely of speculative operations by large sections of the public. Today the volume of such operations is relatively

drastic measures in a long-overdue attempt to restore confidence. And even those measures were relaxed too soon.

There is every justification for intervening in forward exchanges in order to regulate the international flow of funds either as an alternative device to Bank rate changes or in order to make Bank rate changes more effective, always provided that the movements of funds are not due to a perennial balance of payments deficit which calls for measures to affect the basic trend of the domestic economy. There is indeed justification for intervention against purely speculative pressure — always provided that the authorities are genuinely satisfied that the pressure is not justified. It is even arguable that pressure resulting from a lengthening of leads and lags would justify intervention on the ground that such lengthening merely defers the date of receipts and puts forward the dates of payments without altering their totals, so that the authorities are entitled to bridge the time-lag by means of fictitious forward exchange operations. The same argument might even be applied to intervention in order to offset the effect of hedging against foreign direct investments, to the extent to which the authorities feel safe in assuming that these transactions would be self-liquidating, because buyers of forward exchanges sold by authorities are most unlikely to sell their investments — even though they might repatriate their liquid resources.

But it is always difficult to form a reliable opinion about the nature of selling pressure on a currency. If it is persistent the authorities are well advised to try to eliminate the cause rather than camouflage the effect. It is true, measures to that end necessarily take time, and there is every justification to resort to forward tactics to gain time for the elaboration and application of such measures. What is entirely unjustified is to carry official short positions in foreign exchange for years on end, serving in part at least the purpose of meeting a balance of payments deficit, and increasing the commitments as and when additional deficits arise. This is what was done by the British authorities in 1964–67 and for such a policy there can be no excuse.

CHAPTER TWENTY-THREE

EXCHANGE CONTROL

THE defence of an exchange in face of adverse pressure may assume the form of adopting or tightening exchange control. That was the method adopted during the last war in practically every country. Free dealings in foreign exchanges were suspended and all authorised transactions had to be done through banks acting as agents to the authorities. Official rates for the principal exchanges were fixed at the beginning of the war and were left practically unaltered for the duration and for some years after.

Notwithstanding this extreme form of exchange control which was enforced more or less efficiently in Britain and in a number of other countries, exchanges were not immune from attacks after the cessation of hostilities. Britain experienced foreign exchange crises in 1947, 1949 and 1951. The crisis of 1947 was due to the grossly premature resumption of the convertibility of foreign balances in London, surely one of the most incomprehensibly ill-advised acts of foreign exchange policy of all time. There was an acute world-wide scarcity in dollars, so that foreign holders of sterling hastened to convert their holdings into much-needed dollars while the going was good. In a few weeks the Government was forced to suspend convertibility, having lost the bulk of the proceeds of the recently concluded gigantic American loan.

In 1949 strong and widespread anticipation of a devaluation of sterling induced foreigners to keep down sterling holdings. What was much more important, it induced British importers and exporters or their foreign business partners to lengthen leads and lags. The resulting decline in the reserve induced the Government to devalue sterling in spite of repeated emphatic official disclaimers of any intention to do so. In 1951

the outgoing Labour Government took no measures to check
the selling pressure on sterling, but the incoming Conservative
Government imposed drastic import restrictions in addition to
other measures. At the same time, however, it reopened the
foreign exchange market while retaining a series of exchange
restrictions.

In France, too, the maintenance of fairly advanced exchange
controls failed to prevent a succession of foreign exchange
crises during the 'forties and 'fifties. This was due in part to
the inefficient enforcement of the controls which were widely
evaded, but mainly to domestic inflation leading to an extensive
flight of capital, and to political instability.

Towards the end of the 'fifties exchange controls were relaxed
in Western Europe and elsewhere. Even during the 'sixties,
however, there was hardly any country entirely free of exchange
control, although its extent varied between total control in
communist countries where evasion remained a capital offence
and voluntary restrictions in some Western countries. From
time to time during foreign exchange crises most Governments
reinforce their exchange controls. For instance in 1957 the
British Government reimposed controls on sterling credits
financing trade between foreign countries and on sterling credits
for re-financing transactions beyond the customary periods for
which they are financed.

In 1964 it was widely expected that the Socialist victory at
the British election would be followed by an immediate tightening of exchange control in face of the strong selling pressure
on sterling. But although controls are in accordance with
Socialist philosophy, the extent to which they were resorted to
throughout the prolonged crisis was remarkably small. What
is even more remarkable, although there was mounting pressure
by Government supporters in 1966–67 in favour of a relaxation
of the squeeze and the freeze there was hardly any pressure in
favour of replacing those unpopular measures by exchange
control as the principal means of defending sterling.

The main argument against resorting to exchange control is
similar to the argument against defending the exchange against

selling pressure by means of running down reserves, borrowing abroad, or realising foreign assets — it does not deal with the basic causes of the crisis but merely tries to suppress the symptoms produced by the causes. Under the cover of exchange control, inflation can be pursued with impunity for a long time. That is to say, punishment for it is confined to the domestic sphere. The disequilibrium responsible for the pressure on the exchange becomes further accentuated in the absence of corrective measures. The situation becomes increasingly artificial, so that controls of increasing severity have to be applied in order to safeguard the balance of payments against the natural effect of a growing disequilibrium.

An exchange maintained with the aid of exchange control can inspire no full confidence. Even if foreign balances remained exempted from the control their amounts are apt to be reduced from time to time to the indispensable minimum, because of the possibility of extending the control to cover these balances, and also of the possibility that the Government might decide to devalue eventually, in order to be able to restore free exchanges. Moreover, there is bound to develop a black market, if not in the country concerned, at any rate abroad, and rates quoted there are liable to present an exaggerated picture of the extent of the disequilibrium, which again accentuates the distrust.

It is difficult for a democratic country to establish and maintain watertight exchange control in time of peace. The existence of exchange control is likely to induce residents to find loopholes through which to evade it, and the outflow of capital tends to reduce the reserve in spite of restrictions and in spite of official efforts to maintain an even balance between imports and exports. This latter aim can be approached also by means of import controls, quotas, bilateral trading arrangements or other means, such as the 15 per cent surcharge imposed in Britain in 1964 or the import deposits adopted in 1968.

The defence of an exchange against selling pressure by means of import deposits or import surcharges has the disadvantage of provoking retaliations that are liable to wipe out at least part of the beneficial effect of import controls on the exchange. Moreover, since sooner or later they have to be repealed, the possibility of an eventual sudden increase of imports after their removal is looked upon as a potential cause of selling pressure on the exchange.

The trend towards liberalisation of foreign exchange became reversed towards the end of 1969. In the United States earlier 'guidelines' to discourage the outflow of capital were reinforced by statutory provisions. In Britain limits to banks' foreign exchange commitments came to be enforced more strictly. France reverted to tight controls after the disturbances of 1968. Optimistic expectations of an early disappearance of controls as effective means for avoiding or mitigating crises faded out completely.

Prolonged exchange control, import control and application of bilateral trading methods are bound to make the situation increasingly artificial. Under the protection of these devices domestic inflation may proceed unhampered. Indeed that protection provides a high degree of temptation to yield to pressures in favour of overspending. When the Government comes to the conclusion eventually that it can no longer delay the adjustment of exchange parities to its purchasing power parities, the degree of adjustment called for by the situation is bound to be very drastic. The longer the artificial means of defence are applied the larger and the more painful the eventual adjustment will have to be.

F 2

CHAPTER TWENTY-FOUR

DEVALUATION

NEEDLESS to say, devaluation is not a method of defending an exchange but of abandoning its defence. The reason why in spite of this it is included in our list is that it is one method of solving a foreign exchange crisis. Indeed it is one of the few methods by which a foreign exchange crisis can be brought to an end with a stroke of the pen. Most other devices take time to produce their effect, even though their adoption might inspire the market immediately with confidence towards the exchange under pressure. But a devaluation, provided that its extent is considered sufficient, is liable to convert a sweeping selling pressure into an equally sweeping buying pressure through all-round covering of short positions.

When the extent of the disequilibrium that is responsible for the foreign exchange crisis is very considerable devaluation might be the only reasonable answer. As the Macmillan Report stated in 1931, when disequilibrium between price levels exceeds a certain limit it would be inexpedient to try to correct it by means of deflation, for the game would not be worth the candle. The extent of the punishment that would have to be inflicted on the economy by the overdose of deflation required for correcting a major imbalance might be too severe and it might raise even more problems than it would solve.

The Bretton Woods agreement and the IMF rules based on it provide for the possibility of adjusting exchange parities in cases of fundamental disequilibrium. Member Governments are entitled to make changes of up to 10 per cent on either side of their original parities, without having to obtain the Fund's consent. Devaluation beyond that limit has to be negotiated with the Fund. But in practice there is no limit to the member Governments' power to change their parities. If they reach the conclusion that a substantial devaluation is a vital necessity they are in a position to act in disregard of the Fund's disapproval. Judging by past experience, they are not likely to be expelled, and the penalty of refusing any further aid by the IMF would present no immediate problem, because a substantial devaluation would reverse the selling pressure on their currency, at any rate for a time. So the Fund has really no choice but to accept what it is not in a position to prevent.

The reason why devaluations of the leading currencies have been relatively infrequent since the establishment of the IMF lies not in the largely illusory power of the IMF to prevent them but in the reluctance of the Governments themselves to resort to that desperate method of solving their foreign exchange crises. Indeed it may be said without too much exaggeration that the IMF parities are almost as rigid in practice as the gold parities had been under the gold standard.

This rigidity of parities is subject to much criticism. Some of those in favour of solving the problem of the perennial sterling crisis by a drastic devaluation employ the argument that in many instances devaluation did help in the 'thirties. They fail to realise the fundamental difference between conditions as they were then and as they are now, and that we have now to contend with a totally different set of difficulties from those prevailing in the 'thirties.

During the 'thirties devaluation was the answer to the problem in a world suffering from deflation. It was essential to check and reverse the downward trend of world prices, and to that end an all-round devaluation was essential. From the point of view of individual countries devaluations were often needed in order to avoid importing more deflation from countries where deflation had proceeded further or which had devalued to such extent that their exchanges became undervalued. Such countries were in a position to export unemployment by underselling their rivals even in the latter's domestic markets. In many instances the degree of deflation that would have been necessary to prevent this would have been more than the economy of the country could have stood. In any

case, amidst the prolonged depression most Governments had
lost their taste for more deflation.

During the 'sixties there was no falling trend in world
prices to counteract, nor was there in most countries any unemployment to export with the aid of 'exchange dumping'
made possible by deliberately excessive devaluations.   Most
countries had relatively little spare capacity to enable them to
increase their total output as a result of increasing their exports
through underselling their rivals with the aid of their undervalued exchanges. We saw in Chapter 19 that in fully employed
economies any artificial increase of exports is liable to defeat
its object — at any rate as far as the country as a whole is
concerned. While individual industries may benefit the effect
of the increase of their exports would be offset by a corresponding increase in the country's imports. In any case, there can
be no certainty that an increase in the volume of exports
brought about by a devaluation would fully compensate the
country for the disadvantages of an adverse change in the
terms of trade. It would be enabled to sell cheaper in terms of
currencies which have not been devalued, but the increase in
the quantity of its exports may not be sufficient to offset the
fall in their value per unit.

Another fundamental difference between pre-war and post-
war basic economic conditions is that amidst post-war conditions of full employment wages and prices are liable to adapt
themselves much more quickly to the reduced international
value of a devalued currency than they did amidst pre-war
conditions of under-employment. In the 'thirties high unemployment prevented or delayed the upward adjustment of
wages following on devaluations. Such rising trends of prices
as were followed by devaluations were slow and hesitant. Indeed, devaluations exhausted most of their inflationary effects
by checking the downward trend of prices.

On the other hand, owing to the high level of employment
since the war, and especially in the 'sixties, workers would be
in a position in most industrial countries to step up their wage
demands following on devaluations well in excess of the extent

of the price increases that would result from the devaluations. It is true in itself a reduction of the international value of a currency does not necessarily entail a rise in wages. But since it causes an increase in the prices of imported goods and therefore an increase in the cost of living, wage demands follow devaluations like night follows day.

Nor would the extent of wage increases be confined to the adjustment of wages to the high cost of living. The stimulus given by a devaluation to an already over-employed economy would further strengthen the bargaining power of trade unions. While before a devaluation the Governments are forced to pursue deflationary policies in defence of their parities, the reversal of the trend of foreign exchanges as a result of the devaluation would make squeeze and wage restraint unnecessary, at any rate until prices have adapted themselves to the reduced international value of the currency. In the absence of squeeze and restraint employers, too, are liable to give way even more easily to wage demands, if only to avoid being prevented by strikes from taking full advantage of the short-lived boom that follows a devaluation.

The technical foreign exchange situation itself undergoes an instantaneous change for the better as a result of a devaluation — always provided that the extent of the cut is not only sufficient but is deemed to be sufficient by the market. A devaluation which is deemed, rightly or wrongly, to be inadequate, is liable to aggravate selling pressure on the exchange, because the market will anticipate a second instalment. This happened in 1967 when sterling was devalued by 14 per cent and again in 1969 when the French franc was devalued by 11 per cent. Moreover it is only the first step that is difficult. The fact that a Government has proved itself unwilling or unable to defend the parity with the last drop of its blood and devalued in spite of repeated solemn promises not to, shows that it does not regard parities as sacrosanct. Speculators and others who make a profit on the devaluation derive much encouragement from it.

But if the extent of the devaluation is deemed to be adequate all short positions will be covered at once. Indeed since the currency concerned comes to be considered absolutely secure on its lower level some long positions are liable to be created in it against currencies which are deemed to be next on the list of devaluations.   This is even more the case if the extent of the devaluation is deemed to be excessive, so that its partial revaluation is considered a possibility.   In any case an excessive devaluation of a major currency is liable to cause selling pressure on other currencies.

As and when the undervaluation of the exchange disappears through a rise in domestic prices or a fall in prices abroad, or through devaluations of other currencies, the foreign exchange position is liable to change for worse once more.   The currency concerned is liable to be regarded once more as devaluation-prone.   Since before a devaluation all Governments pledge themselves emphatically against devaluation, any new promise that the new parity would be defended would carry no con-viction.   The more frequently the devaluation is repeated the less official pledges not to repeat it would be trusted.   So a devalued currency's immunity to crises is liable to be of relatively short duration.

The extent and duration of the advantages derived by the balance of payments from a devaluation depends largely on the various 'elasticities' that determine the response of supply of and demand for the exports of the devaluing country, and for the imports of the non-devaluing countries.   We have already alluded to the interplay of exchange rates and terms of trade after a devaluation.   What is equally important is the extent to which exporters of the devaluing countries are in a position to take advantage of their improved opportunities through increasing the volume of their exports, and the extent to which demand abroad for their goods responds to the lower prices in terms of the importing countries' currencies.   Much depends on whether there is a buyers' market or a sellers' market in the principal goods exported and imported, also on how supplies of goods which could be substituted for the goods in question react to the change.

A great deal has been written since the war about this aspect

of the subject.   Much of the literature on 'elasticities' is quite
distinctly biased.   Those in favour of devaluations (or, for that
matter, of floating exchanges) are inclined to be elasticity-
optimists or elasticity-pessimists according to the way it suits
their argument against fixed parities.   The truth of the matter
is that every change of parity is a leap in the dark, as there is
no possible way of predicting how the various elasticities would
operate.   Any pretence at being able to do more than intelli-
gently guessing on the basis of the unpredictable degrees to
which even such influences which are predictable would operate
ought to be treated with the contempt that such pseudo-
scholarly attempts to mislead the reader deserve.

Owing to the fundamental difference between pre-war deflationary mass unemployment and post-war inflationary over-
employment, the argument in favour of devaluation on the
ground of its favourable results before the war is quite untenable.
It is as if a doctor prescribed a medicine for high blood-pressure
on the ground that the self-same medicine had proved its worth
when used against low blood-pressure.

Both the British devaluation of 1967 and the French devaluation of 1969 have proved that unless that act is followed
by national regeneration and by a series of tough deflationary
measures — as it was in 1931 — it is doomed to failure.   If it
merely accentuates the prevailing inflation by making it easier
to proceed, the defence of a currency at its lower parity is
liable to become an additional source of crisis.

CHAPTER TWENTY-FIVE

FLOATING EXCHANGES

FREQUENT repetition of devaluations and revaluations as and when it is deemed expedient in face of a persistent selling or buying pressure constitutes a system of flexible exchanges. The Bretton Woods system was originally intended by some of its authors and supporters to establish such a system. In practice, as we saw in the last chapter, most countries availed themselves of their rights under the rules of the IMF to change their parities very sparingly, if at all. Even the widely canvassed idea of widening the spread between the maximum and minimum support points, so as to allow a wider fluctuation of the rates within those limits, has not been accepted. On the contrary, most monetary authorities fixed their official support points within less than the maximum limits permitted under IMF rules and maintain their actual exchange rate usually well within the support points of their own choice.

There has been much agitation in favour of a substantial broadening of the spread between support points, as a means to enable monetary authorities to defend their parities more effectively against both selling or buying pressure. It is firmly believed by a school of thought of considerable importance that wider limits to fluctuations would assist in the defence of the exchange, because the possibility of wide exchange movements tends to increase the risk attached to speculation in anticipation of changes in parities. If the support points are at $\frac{3}{4}$ per cent of the parity on each side then an exchange which is depressed to its minimum support point as a result of selling pressure can only recover to the extent of $1\frac{1}{2}$ per cent. That $1\frac{1}{2}$ per cent, plus the discount on the forward exchange, constitutes the maximum of possible losses by speculators who sell short.

Many people hold the view that the risk of such a relatively

moderate loss is not sufficient deterrent to speculators who
expect to make a profit many times larger if their expectation
of a devaluation should materialise. They advocate much
wider support points in order that the risk should be heavier,
also in order to give the authorities more manœuvring space
for squeezing speculators. But the same effect can be achieved
without tampering with support points, by allowing forward
margins to widen instead of keeping them artificially narrow by
means of official support.

If exchange rates are permitted to float within a range of,
say, 5 per cent or 10 per cent instead of their present *de facto*
range of 1½ per cent in the case of most of the leading exchanges,
there is a better chance for the excess or deficiency of supply in
relation to demand to find normal counterparts through a free
operation of the market mechanism. This would not necessarily protect, however, the reserves from crises through devaluation scares. Once an exchange has come to be looked
upon as devaluation-prone one-sided selling pressure tends to
depreciate it, in the absence of official intervention, to its
minimum support points, no matter at what level that support
point is fixed. It is true, speculators who do not expect an
early devaluation and are willing to provide a counterpart to
speculative selling if profit prospects make it appear worth their
while are more likely to take a risk if the wide margin between
minimum and maximum support points offers the possibility
of a relatively large profit than they are in existing conditions
in which the maximum of possible profit is limited to 1½ per cent
plus the forward discount. Nevertheless, during acute devaluation scares the majority of speculators would be selling and the
bulk of the counterpart to their sales would have to be provided
by the authorities, no matter where the support points are fixed.

The fact that in most instances the authorities defend their
spot rates at a level above the minimum support point and that
they maintain the forward margins artificially narrow seems to
indicate that, on the basis of their extensive practical experience, they do not believe in the argument in favour of widening
the spread between support points. This does not, of course,

necessarily mean that they are right, but it is a consideration worth bearing in mind in judging the opposite view that is so firmly held by many economists who have not had the benefit of practical experience.

Another school of thought that includes a large number of well-known monetary economists is not content with a substantial widening of the spread between support points, but advocates the complete abolition of parities and support points, so as to allow exchanges 'to find their true level'. According to them, whenever there is selling pressure on an exchange it should be allowed to produce its effect unhampered by support points or by official intervention. Those who hold this view have a faith, bordering on superstition, in the existence of an ideal exchange rate at which supply and demand, if allowed free play, always result in equilibrium of imports and exports. They also believe in the existence of a symmetric system under which yielding to buying pressure tends to produce the same long-range effect as yielding to selling pressure. Finally, their faith implies a belief that exchange movements are always the effect of previous changes in relative price levels or in balances of payments and are never the cause of such changes. All three assumptions are entirely false.

The same degree of excess demand for foreign exchanges is liable to change the rates to widely different degrees according to the mood of the market and the sense in which the market is basically biased. Movements produced by excess demand are liable to become self-aggravating and the depreciation of the national exchange, instead of producing an automatic corrective effect, tends to increase the volume of demand for foreign exchanges and to create additional selling by speculators and others. In given circumstances a depreciating exchange appears to the market even less attractive after its depreciation than it had appeared before its depreciation which is supposed to have corrected its disequilibrium. Its downward trend, so far from attracting additional supplies, tends to increase the volume of selling and to reduce the volume of buying.

determination and ability to hold those parities, for there would be no parities to the defence of which they are committed. The defence of an exchange at a rate which commands no confidence might well prove to be even costlier than its defence at its minimum support points under the system of fixed parities. Its defence with the aid of supporting the forward rate might become more difficult, if not impossible, because, as a result of the considerably increased commercial and hedging demand for forward exchange facilities under a system of floating exchanges, the market might become saturated.

So far from preventing foreign exchange crises, the system of floating exchanges would create such crises more frequently and the intensity of such crises would be no less than under fixed parities. This was the experience with floating exchanges between the wars. Unfortunately the post-war generation of economists is unfamiliar with the grave inconveniences of that system, and the crises of today are always more harassing than the crises of past periods. Yet between the two wars the world suffered more through excessive flexibility of exchanges than through their excessive rigidity when defended at fixed parities. Nor is the post-war experience of Canada and other countries with floating exchanges exactly encouraging. At any rate the Governments directly concerned did not think so, judging by their decisions to return to fixed parities.

The latest fashion in flexibility is the system of the 'crawling peg', under which parities and support points, instead of being subject to occasional substantial changes, would be adapted gradually over a period of years. No conceivable system could be so utterly devoid of common sense. Its advocates seem to imagine that if speculators and others assume, rightly or wrongly, that sterling is overvalued by 10 per cent, they would patiently abstain from operating on that assumption for five years while the exchange is adapted at the rate of 2 per cent p.a. Quite on the contrary, the initiation of the 'crawl' would amount to official admission that the existing parities need adjusting, and this would stimulate speculative pressure.

CHAPTER TWENTY-SIX

RAISING THE PRICE OF GOLD

ONE of the widely canvassed devices for preventing foreign exchange crises is to increase the amount of international reserves. Suggestions that this can be done by means of creating some form of international credit unit that should be accepted in settlement of balance of payments deficit will be dealt with in the next chapter. In the present chapter we shall deal with the much simpler suggestion to achieve the desired end by raising the price of gold. The most popular formula to that effect is that the United States should double the dollar price of gold and that all other member countries of the IMF should adjust their gold parities accordingly. The result would be an increase in the book value of all gold reserves by 100 per cent. The addition to the total international reserves would be equal to the present dollar equivalent of the world's monetary stock of gold.

This formula has a great advantage over the various liquidity schemes. The additional liquid reserve created through its adoption would be gold and not some fictitious book-keeping entry. From this point of view there is indeed much to recommend it. On the other hand, the distribution of the additional resources would be quite unsatisfactory. Countries which already hold large reserves would increase their reserves considerably, while countries with small net gold reserves would hardly benefit by it at all. Britain has a small gold reserve but would benefit through an increase in the value of her investments in the gold-mining industry.

Yet the main purpose of those pressing for additional international liquid reserves is precisely to assist countries with inadequate reserves. Most of the agitation in favour of urgent action to that end always comes, in fact, from such countries. It is always the monetary authorities who actually need such additional reserves or who anticipate a continued decline of their reserves to danger level who contend that the existing quantity of monetary gold is not sufficient for meeting increased and increasing requirements. This theory will be discussed in the next chapter. For our present purpose it is sufficient to point out that under the proposal of raising the price of gold the 'have-not' countries would not get sufficient additional resources and their exchanges would continue to be exposed to crises just as before.

Admittedly, the countries with large gold reserves would be placed in a better position as a result of a revaluation of gold to lend to countries with inadequate reserves. This was in fact what M. Jacques Rueff, a persistent advocate of gold revaluation, had in mind. Whether the chief beneficiaries from gold revaluation would in fact become liberal in placing their additional resources at the disposal of other countries is quite another matter. It is arguable that such increased assistance would mean a further increase of the foreign debt burden of the borrowing countries. In the absence of such additional facilities they might have made an effort to balance their account and to ensure that it does not become unbalanced again. But the easier availability of external support would provide both temptation and opportunity for taking the line of least resistance, even if it meant an addition to their international short-term indebtedness which would have to be repaid sooner or later.

Whether or not the grand total of liquid resources covers the grand total of world requirements, deficit countries are bound to be short of liquid resources if their deficits are substantial and persistent. It is arguable that, without painful devices to restore the balance of their economies, any conceivable increase in their liquid reserves would only provide temporary protection for their exchanges against adverse pressure. The perennial adverse balance would deplete any additional resources in due course, and the position would then be worse than before the receipt of the additional resources, because the country would have to face an additional foreign debt.

As we shall try to prove in the next chapter, it stands to reason that the addition to the volume of international liquid reserves would weaken the resistance of Governments to inflation. The net result of the change would be, therefore, an acceleration of the rise in prices, so that in due course the surplus liquidity would be offset by the increase in requirements resulting from higher prices. The argument applies of course also to an increase of liquidity through raising the price of gold.

Advocates of that device argue that a doubling of the price of gold would not mean an automatic doubling of price levels. Nobody could seriously suggest that prices would adjust themselves immediately and automatically to the higher money value of gold. If all or most of the important countries were to devalue at the same time and to the same extent then even the cost of their imported goods would not increase automatically. But it is arguable that the feeling that there is now ample scope for further spending sprees and more inflation without tears should not be ignored when considering this aspect of the problem. Any substantial increase in reserves would provide inflationist demagogy with ample opportunities for exerting their influence on public opinion, Parliaments and Governments.

Moreover, the ease with which the problem of obviating foreign exchange crises for a time would be solved with a stroke of the pen would make it very tempting to repeat the operation from time to time. Once the general rise in prices has caught up with the new price of gold that price could be doubled again and again. Anticipation of a repetition of the performance would lead to increased hoarding of gold and of all forms of assets which are liable to increase in price following on revaluations of gold unless the increase is sufficiently impressive to make its early repetition appear unnecessary.

Beyond doubt, the effect of doubling the price of gold would be a mitigation of exchange parity uncertainites, because more resources would become available for defending the existing and without involving further surrender of gold to the IMF.

Under the formula that was eventually agreed upon, subject to ratification, the IMF is to grant member Governments 'Special Drawing Rights' to a maximum to be determined by their respective quotas. The Governments would be in a position to add the amount of their allocation to their published gold and foreign exchange reserve, increasing thereby the potential support to their currencies. The Special Drawing Rights will represent additional liquidity. Central Banks whose exchanges are under pressure will be in a position to sell their holdings of SDR to other Central Banks against the latters' currencies. The buyers will in turn be able to re-sell these SDRs to other Central Banks when their own currency comes under selling pressure.

The use of SDRs is limited to an average of 70 per cent of the allocations over a five-year period. Any member who exceeds that limit will be called upon by the IMF to reduce to that limit the amount of SDRs sold, by re-purchasing the excess. Another limitation to the free use of SDRs is the rule under which holders are not entitled to use it for the purpose of changing the composition of their reserves.

The plan has been adopted for an experimental period of three years, after which its rules will be reconsidered. The total initial amount to be allocated was fixed at $9,500 m., of which $3,500 m. was to be allocated in the first year and $3,000 m. in each of the two subsequent years. SDRs will be distributed as a free gift, and member Central Banks will not have to deposit with the IMF any gold or currencies. Their value will depend wholly on the obligation of members to accept them in exchange for currency.

Governments which originally opposed it were persuaded to agree to the discussion of some international liquidity scheme with the aid of the argument that it would be necessary to have some formula elaborated and agreed upon while the going is good, so as to have it in readiness in case of emergency. There is undoubtedly an ever-present possibility of some major crisis in face of which existing international reserves would be

painfully inadequate.   A slump on the lines of the crises of the
1930s might conceivably develop, especially if non-stop expansion is allowed to continue at an accelerated pace.   Or the
Euro-currency situation might get out of control through a
series of major defaults which would produce grave chain-
reactions.   If and when such a situation should arise, or even
if and when the threat of such developments should become
sufficiently obvious to call for urgent action, it might be too
late to try to embark on lengthy discussions in order to elaborate
an agreed formula.   By the time agreement is reached the
crisis would be certain to assume a self-aggravating character
and the remedies which might have checked it at an earlier
phase would then prove to be ineffective.

Even the most conservative Governments were willing to
accept the above line of reasoning, hence their willingness to
proceed with the elaboration of what was often referred to as a
contingency plan.   By the time that plan emerged, however,
it seemed to have changed its character.   In practice SDRs
have become an inflationary measure pure and simple, enabling
Governments with large import surpluses to defer long-
overdue deflationary measures in order to reduce the deficits
of their visible trade balances and to continue to allow inflation to proceed with impunity.   Since the resulting rise in
world prices will wipe out the additional liquidity, the device
will provide no protection against foreign exchange crises, even
if it will provide some measure of immediate relief.   Is such
relief really necessary in normal conditions?

Now the presence or absence of a scarcity of liquid reserves
is very much a matter of opinion.   According to the Anglo-
Saxon school of thought liquid reserves are already scarce and
have been scarce for years.   According to the opinion widely
held in Western Europe, reserves are excessive and should be
reduced through the elimination of the gold exchange standard,
that is, the termination of the use of the dollar and sterling as
reserve currencies.   This opinion was originally strongly supported by France, but as a result of the deterioration of her
reserve position she has become a borrower and it now suits

of higher prices has been much larger than the extent to which they have been increased as a result of expansion in the volume of international trade. Had prices been kept at their 1939 level, or even at their 1945 level, the existing liquid reserves would be well in excess of normal requirements on the basis of the existing volume of trade and would allow for a considerable increase of that volume.

The reason why world prices have been rising since the end of the war is precisely that there are usually sufficient resources to enable deficit countries to finance their deficits without having to resort to sufficiently drastic deflationary measures to check the inflationary world trend effectively. All the time as the complaints about the inadequacy of reserves have been becoming increasingly insistent prices have been rising. There have been sufficient resources available to enable various deficit countries to deal with the foreign exchange crises without having to resort to a degree of deflation that would effectively check and reverse the upward trend for a few years.

Had the additional liquid reserves, agitation for which had become increasingly vocal, actually existed in 1964, the Labour Government might not have bothered to adopt any of the defensive measures it felt impelled to adopt gradually under the pressure of the recurrent crises. It would have increased its own expenditure even more, and it would not have made any real efforts to check the wage inflation. It would have embarked on additional egalitarian measures which, by raising the level of lower incomes and reducing the level of higher incomes, would have produced a strongly inflationary effect at a time when there was no economic justification for it. Overfull-employment would have further increased and would have further strengthened the bargaining position of trade unions. Non-stop inflationary boom would have created many more unsound positions in business. Possibly by now we might have reached the stage of disillusionment as a result of a slump on pre-war lines.

The above arguments are not intended for making out a case against the adoption of some liquidity scheme which would

G

really be kept in readiness in order to be applied in case of a major international financial or economic crisis. But there is of course always a temptation as well as an opportunity that once a formula has been agreed upon it should be applied even in the absence of any major emergency that would justify its application, just for the sake of making things more comfortable. Whether the Governments concerned would be sufficiently statesmanlike to bear in mind that, by using up the additional resources unnecessarily, these would cease to be available to meet a major crisis, is of course anybody's guess. It is important that the more conservative monetary authorities should reserve their veto to prevent a misuse of the scheme.

The possibility of a liquidity scheme and the publicity attached to the discussions about it is to blame to some extent for the inadequacy of the defensive measures adopted by the U.K. and U.S. Governments to ensure a surplus on their balance of payments.   Both Governments ought to have realised the need for policies which would have not only restored the equilibrium of their balance of payments and maintained it precariously but would have ensured an adequate safety margin to prevent a recurrence of foreign exchange crises.   Unfortunately both Governments seemed to rely on hopes of being able to borrow more in the distant future, thanks to the adoption of SDR and an increase in their amount.

It is precisely because such hopes were entertained that neither of the Governments seemed to be concerned sufficiently with the outlook of their exchanges in the long run. In anticipation of a windfall in the form of additionally created international borrowing facilities to meet their perennial deficit, the U.S. authorities delayed the adoption of effective measures for damping down domestic consumer demand until 1969, by which time a growing deficit on their visible trade came to aggravate their burden of military and economic aid abroad and their export of capital. Even then the effect of the deflationary measures came to be mitigated by large-scale borrowing abroad. The British Government, too, deferred until 1969 the adoption of effective squeeze measures, hoping that external aid might obviate the necessity for applying painful remedies. For this reason, sterling and even the dollar remained more exposed to crises than they would have been if the Governments had relied on their own strength rather than on hopes of additional borrowing facilities created with the aid of liquidity schemes.

The above arguments do not lose their force merely because during the second half of 1969 Britain managed to improve her balance of payments. For the very fact of that improvement, reinforced by the optimism generated by the availability of SDR, is certain to make it even more difficult for the Government to resist wage inflation. One of the manifestations of Parkinson's Law is that the availability of means for financing a trade deficit leads to the creation of a deficit to be financed.

CHAPTER TWENTY-EIGHT

JOINING THE
COMMON MARKET .

THE present chapter deals with a device to meet foreign exchange crises by enlisting the support of a group of countries with which the country concerned has entered or wishes to enter into special relationship. Although Britain and the Common Market provide an outstanding instance of this proposed method of defence, similar relationships are of course conceivable between other countries.

When Mr Wilson announced in November 1966 that, contrary to his previous declared policy to which he pledged himself at the general election in March 1966, he was now keen on joining the Common Market, in the absence of any explanation of why he had changed his mind it came to be suspected by General de Gaulle and others that his volte-face was inspired by his desire to ensure for sterling the support of the Western European countries. However this may be, from the time of the announcement of that decision the ups and downs of the chances of joining the Common Market, as assessed by the foreign exchange market, came to play an important part among the influences affecting sterling.

The reasons why it was widely assumed that joining the Common Market would be an effective remedy for the sterling crisis are the following :

(1) The last few years witnessed a remarkable redistribution of monetary gold reserves as between the U.S. and Western Europe. France, Germany and Italy have accumulated substantial reserves, while the once impregnable reserve of the U.S. declined by half in ten years. At the same time, the technical position of the

dollar was also weakened by a spectacular increase in the volume of foreign dollar balances and the perennial deficit on the American balance of payments continued to press on the dollar and on the reserve. In such circumstances it was deemed necessary to envisage the moment when the U.S. would no longer be willing, or indeed able, to bolster up sterling. For this reason, it appears advisable to ensure that sterling would be looked after by the countries of the Common Market.

(2) All free trader elements in British opinion — whether Conservatives, Liberals or Socialists — welcomed the idea of joining the Common Market as on the basis of their free trader philosophy they assumed that it would mean salvation for sterling. They firmly believed in the absolute advantages of being able to rely on a large market with a high purchasing power. They took it for granted that the resulting stronger competition would make British industries more efficient and would enable them to take full advantage of the increased possibilities of exporting to Western Europe.

(3) Even though it was vaguely assumed that joining the Common Market might necessitate the abandonment of Commonwealth preference and would place British agriculture at a disadvantage, and that the Sterling Area might have to be dissolved, they assumed that the gains from increasing exports to the Common Market would more than outweigh the losses.

This optimistic view of the advantages to be derived from joining was not held unanimously by a long way. Opponents of the idea based their opposition mainly on the following arguments :

(1) The British balance of payments was bound to suffer a considerable initial loss as a result of joining the Common Market. Estimates, for what they are worth, assess that loss at between £175 m. and £400 m. p.a., a deficit which the balance of payments could ill afford.

(2) It was feared that the virtual disbanding of the Common-wealth for the sake of joining the Common Market would entail the termination of the Sterling Area. This would mean heavy withdrawals by official holders of sterling reserves, who would want to diversify their reserves and would no longer feel bound to sterling by ties of loyalty. Indeed some Sterling Area countries might want to withdraw their reserves altogether. The amount of privately held Sterling Area sterling balances would also decline as a result of the decline of trade with the Commonwealth.

(3) Opponents of the idea of joining the Common Market were by no means certain that the trade balance between Britain and the Common Market countries would benefit by the change. Apart altogether from the effect on agricultural imports, it was feared that the opening of the British market to Western European industrial goods would increase Britain's import surplus rather than reduce it.

(4) The joining of the Common Market was considered at best irrelevant from the point of view of defending sterling. It was felt that hopes of miraculous results would provide yet another excuse for deferring any genuine effort to work out our own salvation by means of our own exertions. The view was held that the only thing that really mattered was to induce the British worker to work harder, and that if this could be done Britain would be bound to prosper, in or out of the Common Market. On the other hand, if the British worker could not be induced to work harder Britain would be fated to decline, in or out of the Common Market, though it was feared she would decline faster in the Common Market, owing to her being more exposed to competition. It is true, supporters of the Common Market argue that competition would force British industries to become more efficient. The answer to that argument is that no industry in the Common Market would be so fully exposed to international competition as shipbuilding and

shipping is even with Britain outside the Common Market, and yet, in spite of this, these two industries are among the least efficient industries in Britain.

It seems probable that, on balance, an improvement in the prospects of joining the Common Market was a bear point for sterling rather than a bull point. What is more, even prolonged negotiations to that end were expected to be liable to precipitate and aggravate a sterling crisis owing to its effect on the attitude of Sterling Area countries. Their authorities were well aware that Britain would be unable to pay out their sterling balances in gold or in dollars, so they might withdraw their balances from London while the going is good. These fears were greatly mitigated by the guarantees arranged in 1968.

A disintegration of the Sterling Area would entail incalculable consequences also through its effect on leads and lags. A foretaste of this was provided by the experience of 1967, when the currencies of many Sterling Area countries were not devalued with sterling. Once the Sterling Area ceases to exist importers and exporters could no longer rely on the stability of sterling in relation to the former Sterling Area currencies. How leads and lags would be affected depends on whether sterling would command more confidence than the other former Sterling Area currencies. Should it come to be assumed that Britain's admission into the Common Market would be made conditional on a devaluation of sterling, or that a deterioration of her trade balance after her admission in the Common Market might force her to devalue, countries of the former Sterling Area might adjust their leads and lags to the detriment of sterling. Owing to the large volume of the trade involved, such lengthening of leads and lags might well make a difference of several hundreds of millions of pounds.

Conversely, it is conceivable that sterling would command more confidence than the former Sterling Area currencies, or at any rate some of them. To the extent to which that would be the case, leads and lags would change in favour of sterling.

Taking everything into consideration the initial effect of joining the Common Market would be decidedly detrimental to sterling.   Fears that a devaluation might be made one of the conditions for Britain's admission into the Common Market subsided after recent changes of parities.   Even allowing for this and for the other considerations the possibility of joining the Common Market is more likely to aggravate sterling's difficulties than cure them.   Even the most enthusiastic supporters of joining the Common Market only claim that sterling would stand to benefit by it in the long run.   Yet the foreign exchange market is primarily concerned with prospects in the short run.

CHAPTER TWENTY-NINE

COMPULSORY INVESTMENT-HEDGING

THE remedies described in Chapters 17 to 28 are all well known and the arguments for and against their application have been widely discussed over a period of years. The present chapter, on the other hand, has received no publicity apart from my article in the *Guardian* on the morning of the devaluation in 1967. I am only too well aware that its application would not solve the basic problem and might even make it easier for the Government of the day to defer the supreme effort needed for achieving such a basic solution. It was for this reason that I hesitated for years before deciding, not without grave misgivings, to communicate my plan to the Treasury in June 1967.

I reached that decision under the influence of the acute sterling crisis that developed during the first days of the war in the Middle East. It looked for a short time as if the defences of sterling were in danger of breaking down as a result of the effect of the embargo on oil shipments to Britain by the Arab countries and of a wholesale withdrawal of their sterling balances. Although sterling recovered from the effects of the Arab–Israeli war, it developed fresh weakness in the autumn and was devalued in November. I am convinced that this costly devaluation could have been avoided if the compulsory investment-hedging scheme had been adopted.

The substance of my plan was that the Treasury should be given powers to order U.K. residents holding investments in non-sterling countries to hedge against such investments by selling forward a corresponding amount of the foreign currencies concerned. The resulting demand for forward sterling would offset to a considerable extent selling pressure due to speculative attacks, wholesale withdrawals of foreign balances, lengthening of leads and lags, and hedging by foreign investors holding investments in the U.K. or the Sterling Area.

Even if the application of the device were confined to investments in specified currencies, and even amongst those only to currencies whose forward exchange is at a premium against sterling, the amount of support that could thus be mobilised at short notice would bear comparison with the total of credits, drawing rights and swap facilities obtained by the British authorities from foreign Central Banks and the IMF during 1964–69, or with the Bank of England's short position in dollars resulting from the official support to forward sterling during the same period.

The proposed device would impose no undue hardship on U.K. investors abroad. Since its application would be confined to the compulsory sale of forward exchanges which are at a premium against sterling, investors would make a small profit corresponding to the premium. In so far as the forward transactions could not be arranged through their difficulties as a matter of routine the authorities would have to provide the necessary guarantees. The only disadvantage from the point of view of the investors would be that they would forgo the chance of making a capital profit on a devaluation of sterling. Such a profit would have, however, no moral justification anyhow. And in any case it is not an unreasonable price for investors to put up with some inconvenience in return for the privilege of having been allowed to acquire and hold foreign investments during a period when Britain possessed no export surplus to cover the export of capital, so that such transactions tended to increase the burden on sterling.

This point brings me to the reason why I feel justified in producing my plan in spite of the very real risk that it might be misused by irresponsible Governments for deferring the day when they have to make the country face realities. It is that the same deplorable result might easily be brought about through a compulsory realisation of the foreign investments themselves. This was done in both World Wars, but it is still considered utterly wrong to resort to it in time of peace. Nevertheless, there are indications that the idea is not unfamiliar to the Labour Government. Its leading Ministerial spokesmen repeatedly referred to Britain's foreign investments as 'sterling's second line of defence'. Unless they were toying with the idea of enforcing a realisation of such investments they could not be considered as sterling's second line of defence. There is a growing pressure on the part of the Left wing of the Labour Party to induce the Government to resort to that device as a means of being able to inflate with impunity. In view of the unpopularity of the measures adopted in defence of sterling it would not be surprising if the Government were to choose to abstain, on the occasion of future attacks on sterling, from repeating those measures and defended sterling instead with the proceeds of compulsorily acquired or 'voluntarily' surrendered British foreign investments.

Surely it is beyond dispute that such a measure would inflict incomparably graver hardship on British investors than the minor inconvenience of hedging against a certain percentage of their investments by means of forward exchange transactions that would cost them nothing and would leave them in full possession of their investments. From the point of view of the balance of payments, too, compulsory hedging would mean a slight increase in invisible earnings by the amount of the premiums collected by investors, while a compulsory realisation of the investments would mean a grievous loss of invisible earnings and of capital gains, not to speak of the other advantages of holding such investments.

Admittedly the administration of the proposed device would be more difficult and complicated than the official forward sales of dollars. But the contingent liability represented by the Bank of England's short position in dollars is calculated to inspire distrust abroad because there are no assets whatsoever behind such a short position, while short positions resulting from compulsory investment-hedging are backed by considerable assets of real value.

I am the first to admit that the adoption of my proposed

device would not solve the basic problem of sterling's perennial weakness. But it would be able to reinforce the defences of sterling in order to resist an acute attack and to give the Government time for preparing the necessary defensive measures. Unless such measures are in fact prepared the net result of my proposal, like that of other measures discussed in the previous chapters, would only be a temporary relief, at the cost of an aggravation of the problem in the long run.

CHAPTER THIRTY

NATIONAL REGENERATION

As we saw in the preceding chapters, none of the wide variety of devices that can be applied in face of a foreign exchange crisis can be relied upon for producing a really lasting effect. Some of them are not even expected to do so. The shielding of the domestic economy behind a screen of exchange controls or import controls, the camouflaging of the crisis by external borrowing or by official support of the forward exchange, the stimulation of exports and handicapping of imports by means of devaluations or depreciations, cannot be expected to solve the problem, except perhaps temporarily.

But even genuine and successful deflation and other measures to increase the basic strength of the exchange by restoring a sound balanced economy could bring about only a temporary recovery of the exchange. For once the balance of payments has regained its equilibrium, the causes which had been responsible for bringing about its disequilibrium are apt to be allowed to return in a relatively short time. This was what happened in Britain on every occasion since the war when stop-go was applied. As soon as the measures adopted for damping down the economy have been relaxed or removed, unsound tendencies began once more to rear their ugly heads. In a disheartingly short time the situation was the same as it had been before the remedies came to be applied.

We saw in Chapter 20 that the repetition of this experience on a number of occasions during the two decades from 1945 has gone a long way towards discrediting the stop-go system. It has bred a high degree of fatalism. 'What is the use of trying to remove the overload from the economy at the cost of setbacks and stagnation,' so the argument runs, 'if within a very short time the overload becomes just as heavy as before?'

Which attitude recalls Swift's reply to his servant who would not clean the Dean's boots because anyhow they would soon be dirty again: 'Why should you have breakfast? You would soon be hungry again.' Surely even temporary relief of the overload is better than no relief at all. As we already pointed out in Chapter 20, but for the interruptions caused by stop-go the pace of creeping inflation would have become greatly accelerated long before now. Even so, it would be idle to pretend that the temporary effects produced by stop-go are the answer to foreign exchange crises.

In order to find a solution we must recall our diagnosis in Chapter 16, tracing the basic cause of the crisis to the demoralisation of the British people since the war. If that diagnosis is accepted it points to the obvious remedy — national regeneration.

Such national regenerations occurred since the war in a number of countries. We have heard a great deal about the 'German miracle', the 'Japanese miracle' and the 'Italian miracle'. The three defeated nations staged most remarkable recoveries through national regeneration. The end of the war found these proud nations crushed and humiliated, but in a remarkably short time they succeeded in reconstructing the devastations of the war and in building up strong and stable economies. This was because, to their eternal credit, they succeeded in overcoming the demoralising effects of defeat. They were determined to prove to their own satisfaction and to that of the world that at their best they could be as good as their conquerors. Their supreme national effort in the economic sphere restored their self-respect and earned for them the respect and admiration of other nations. It was the first time that defeated and disarmed nations have regained influence and power, not through military rearmament but through emerging as first-rate industrial powers while maintaining the stability of their currencies to a remarkable degree.

Among the victorious nations, too, France, under General de Gaulle, spurred by the determination to wipe out the memory of her humiliating initial defeat and of the long enemy occupation, succeeded in restoring and strengthening her economy, even though the violent troubles of May–June 1968 resulted in a sharp setback and a lasting deterioration leading to the devaluation of the franc in August 1969. Russia, too, has every reason to be proud of her achievement of physical reconstruction and of industrialisation on an unprecedented scale. Among smaller nations, too, the way in which the Netherlands, for instance, shrugged off her crushing loss of her investments confiscated in Sukarno's Indonesia showed that the Dutch people could still derive inspiration from its proud history.

Britain's history is second to none when it comes to examples of displays of a similar spirit. Yet there is very little in Britain's post-war economic record of which the British people would have cause to be proud. The demoralising effect of welfare state mentality and overfull-employment, aggravated by competitive bribing of the electorate by the rival political parties, have gone a long way towards debasing the once famous British character. Yet twice within the lifetime of the older generation the British character did assert itself. In 1931, confronted with the danger of a collapse of the pound, the British people willingly submitted to the hardships that were imposed upon it, for the sake of emerging from the crisis. And in 1940, in face of the danger of an imminent enemy invasion, the British worker put his back into his work as never before or since in modern times. On both occasions the result was all that could be expected.

Why is it then that after 1945 there was no sign of any national regeneration, of a kind that would have saved Britain from losing the peace after having won the war? In face of the minor crises the sacrifices imposed on the British people were accepted with bad grace and everybody endeavoured to have as little share in them as possible. Was it perhaps because, while in 1931 and in 1940 the threat to the nation was quite obvious, during the late 'forties, in the 'fifties and the 'sixties there was no tangible evidence of it? Most people were doing reasonably well all the time. Unemployment was very small and was at times a negative quantity, the number of vacancies exceeding that of people seeking employment. Although sterling was under severe pressure from time to time on repeated occasions it was rescued thanks to external assistance, with the aid of a minimum of sacrifices, so that British opinion virtually ceased to worry about sterling crises. Something was always bound to turn up.

In any case, during 1964–69 the extent of the run on the pound was largely concealed from the British public, even though in doing so the Government made it more difficult for itself to make the necessary hardships acceptable. All crises were patched up in time, and it was not until a lapse of time that the authorities admitted what a near thing it had been. It is true, there were frequent clarion calls for an increased national effort and for self-restraint. But on every occasion Government spokesmen claimed credit for having succeeded in restoring the economy. They were blowing hot and cold in almost the same breath and their appeal carried no conviction.

I am convinced that, should a really dangerous situation arise, the fine qualities inherent in the British character would assert themselves once more, as they did in 1931 and in 1940. But so long as most people continue to take it for granted that the crisis would be patched up somehow there can be no hope for achieving a national regeneration. Yet without a fundamental change in the attitude of the British people there can be no hope for a lasting recovery of sterling.

National regeneration must begin at the top. So far the Government of the day have signally failed to set an example to be worth following by making a genuine effort to cut down public spending, or even to call a halt to its non-stop increase in good times and in bad. The Government's attitude is quite different to the public sector as against the private sector of the economy. While the squeeze in the latter, though slow to start, came to be pursued effectively in 1969, there was a non-stop increase in the spending spree in the public sector, covered by higher taxes, higher rates and borrowing.

Ample lip-service was paid all along to the need for curtailing public spending, but when it came to the following year's Budgetary estimates the amount was increased on each occasion, not only in terms of pounds, shillings and pence but also in real terms. The increase in public spending was sufficient to wipe out most of the painfully attained results of the squeezes in the private sector. After the devaluation in 1967 the Prime Minister and the Chancellor of the Exchequer appeared to be well aware of the imperative necessity of keeping down public expenditure in order to ensure that the devaluation produced the desired effect on the balance of payments. Yet they were unable to resist pressure by vested Departmental interests. Taxation was increased, although it was bound to step up wage demands and to increase costs of production.

In face of such an example how could the rank and file reasonably be expected to adopt a public-spirited attitude? If Mr Wilson had been half as good at practising the Dunkirk spirit as he was at preaching it he might have encountered a more satisfactory response.

In the continued absence of a national regeneration the outlook for sterling would not be comforting in the long run. Possibly its basic weakness might continue to be patched up again and again with the aid of foreign credits, realisations of foreign assets and sales of essential British industries into foreign ownership. The balance of payments might improve from time to time — through a spreading of the 'English disease'. But there could be no hope for a genuine turn of the tide. Possibly we might even experience short-lived but genuine recoveries from time to time, but in the absence of a national regeneration they could not possibly last.

If only the situation were allowed to deteriorate to an extent that would arouse the dormant good qualities of the British character! Possibly imminence of a collapse of sterling, or the threat of really large-scale unemployment, might produce that effect. But so long as the British public is kept in ignorance of the deterioration of Britain's economic power and influence, so long as that deterioration keeps creeping on insidiously, there is no hope for salvation.

The elimination of the trade deficit, and even the creation of a sufficiently large genuine export surplus to repay the short-term debts created in defence of sterling since 1964, could not be regarded as a solution of the sterling crisis. In all probability it would be back with us in a relatively short time. The British public submitted to the hardships and inconveniences of the defensive measures with the utmost reluctance and under protests. The Government imposed on the nation the measures after very long hesitation and only resorted eventually to compulsion because it was aware of the gravity of the situation which had been concealed from the public. At the flimsiest tentative signs of improvement it hastened to curry favour with the public by relaxing some of the unpopular measures, even though it had repeatedly found that on each occasion the resulting deterioration came to call for the imposition of even harsher measures.

Sterling's repeated temporary recoveries were not brought about by a national regeneration. There was little or no sign of any realisation by the British public of the imperative necessity of making a supreme effort and submitting to hardships. Yet nothing short of a real thorough-going national regeneration could save Britain from relapsing into conditions which it had only been possible to overcome after years of futile experimenting with solutions which would not involve any real sacrifices.

Nothing but a recovery that would justify a feeling that this time the nation has really earned and deserves its emergence from the crisis would generate a spirit of determination not to allow ourselves ever again to drift into a situation which justified our enemies, and even our friends, to look upon Britain as 'the sick man of Europe'. Hard work and much self-restraint is needed before we can live down that reputation. So long as work is looked upon in Germany as a quasi-religious cult while in Britain idleness is looked upon as a quasi-religious cult it is not difficult to predict which nation will make better progress. And anyone who had the opportunity to compare the progress of building operations in Switzerland and in

Britain is bound to agree that Britain is in desperate need of national regeneration.

Taking a long view, it was a misfortune in disguise that, thanks largely to foreign financial assistance and to the conjuring tricks of official forward operations, Britain escaped for so long the punishment her economic demoralisation would have deserved. Whenever such progress as was made was in the right direction, each time it conveyed to the British people the false assurance that Britain was always bound to win the last battle, whether in a shooting war or in the foreign exchange market. Each time the Government succeeded in wallpapering over the cracks, it became even more difficult on the occasion of the next crisis to make the British people realise that it has to work out its own salvation. Yet unless and until that is realised there can be no 'British miracle'. Sterling will remain exposed to frequently recurrent crises.

Having lost her Empire, Britain's only hope to regain her former national greatness lies in the elimination, by her own exertions, of the causes responsible for sterling's basic weakness. If only the British people could be made to realise that, even in the absence of a major national crisis, the danger of a gradual decline is sufficiently grave to call for the display of its finest qualities in the form of hard work and self-denial!

The subject of this chapter is dealt with in much greater detail in my book *Decline and Fall? Britain's Crisis in the Sixties*. It deals specifically with British conditions, which have deteriorated even since I wrote that book in 1968. But demoralisation is not confined to Britain. France, too, has relapsed into the state of political and economic demoralisation from which General de Gaulle rescued her for a period of ten years. There are even indications that the 'German miracle' is drawing near to its conclusion. It is true that in the short run sterling stands to benefit from trouble in other countries. But in the long run demoralisation is infectious, and the spreading of the 'English disease' foreshadows even more foreign exchange crises.

A SELECTED BIBLIOGRAPHY

MONOGRAPHS on individual foreign exchange crises could fill a library. The following list is confined to the books which I found useful in preparing my present book. In addition to the publications listed below, there is much valuable material in the publications of the International Monetary Fund, the Bank for International Settlements and the leading Central Banks, especially the Bank of England, the Federal Reserve Board and the Federal Reserve Bank of New York. For detailed lists of the literature on foreign exchange the reader is referred to the Bibliographies in my *Dynamic Theory of Forward Exchange* and in my *History of Foreign Exchange*.

BLOOMFIELD, ARTHUR I., *Capital Imports and the American Balance of Payments*. Chicago, 1950.
— *Speculative and Flight Movements of Capital in Post-War International Finance*. Princeton, 1954.
BROWN, WEAR M., *External Liquidity of an Advanced Economy*. Princeton, 1964.
CASSEL, GUSTAV, *Money and Foreign Exchange after 1914*. London, 1922.
CHANG, TSE CHUN, *Cyclical Movements in the Balance of Payments*. Cambridge, 1957.
EINZIG, PAUL, *A Dynamic Theory of Forward Exchange* (2nd ed.). London, 1967.
— *The Euro-Dollar System* (4th ed.). London, 1970.
— *The History of Foreign Exchange*. London, 1964.
— *A Textbook on Foreign Exchange* (2nd ed.). London, 1969.
— *Leads and Lags*. London, 1968.
— *The Euro-Bond Market*. London, 1969.
FRAYSINET, PIERRE, *La Politique monétaire de la France, 1924–28*. Paris, 1928.
FRIEDMAN, MILTON, and SCHWARTZ, A. J., *A Monetary History of the United States, 1867–1960*. Princeton, 1963.
GRANT, A. T. K., *The Machinery of Finance and the Management of Sterling*. London, 1967.
GREGORY, SIR THEODORE, *Foreign Exchange before, during and after the War*. Oxford, 1922.

GRUBEL, HERBERT G., *Forward Exchange, Speculation and the International Flow of Capital*. Stanford, 1966.

— *World Monetary Reform*. Oxford, 1964.

HALM, GEORGE N., *The 'Band' Proposal: The Limits of Permissible Exchange Rate Variations*. Princeton, 1965.

HANSEN, BENT, *Foreign Trade Credits and Exchange Reserves*. Amsterdam, 1961.

HARRIS, SEYMOUR, *Exchange Depreciation, its Theory and its History, 1931–35*. Cambridge, Mass., 1936.

— (ed.), *The Dollar in Crisis*. New York, 1961.

HIRSCH, FRED., *Money International*. London, 1967.

KEYNES, J. M., *A Tract on Monetary Reform*. London, 1923.

LEAGUE OF NATIONS, *The International Currency Experience*. Princeton, 1944.

LIPFERT, HELMUT, *Devisenhandel*. Frankfurt, 1958.

MACHLUP, FRITZ, *International Monetary Economics*. London, 1966.

MIKESELL, RAYMOND F., *Foreign Exchange in the Post-War World*. New York, 1954.

MOREAU, ÉMILE, *Souvenirs d'un Gouverneur de la Banque de France*. Paris, 1954.

MORGENSTERN, OSKAR, *International Financial Transactions and Business Cycles*. Princeton, 1959.

NOGARO, BERTRAND, *A Short Treatise on Money and Monetary Systems*. London, 1945.

SEDILLOT, RENÉ, *Le Franc*. Paris, 1953.

— *Du franc Bonaparte au franc de Gaulle*. Paris, 1959.

SHEPHARD, SIDNEY A., *Foreign Exchange in Canada* (3rd ed.). Toronto, 1961.

SOHMEN, EGON, *Flexible Exchange Rates*. Chicago, 1961.

— *The Theory of Forward Exchange*. Princeton, 1966.

U.S. GOVERNMENT PRINTING OFFICE, *The United States Balance of Payments in 1963*. Washington, 1963.

— *The U.S. Balance of Payments*. *Statements by Economists, etc.* Washington, 1963.

WALRÉ DE BORDES, J. VAN, *The Austrian Crown*. London, 1924.

WONNACOTT, PAUL, *The Canadian Dollar, 1948–1962*. Toronto, 1965.

YEAGER, LELAND B., *International Monetary Relations*. New York, 1966.

INDEX

Arbitrage, 11, 15, 84 ff.
Assignats, 92
Automation, 12, 137

Bagehot, Walter, 32
Balance of payments, 13, 19 ff., 33, 64, 66, 81, 105, 131, 148, 152, 168, 173, 182–3, 193, 194
Bank for International Settlements, 126
Bank of England, 26, 62, 65, 68, 87, 127, 144, 147, 149, 150–1, 189, 191
Bank of France, 108
Bank rate, 13, 37, 104, 126, 127, 128, 130, 136, 138–9, 144, 153
Belgian franc, 58
Black market, 156
Board of Trade, 81
Budgetary deficits, 93–4

Capital movements, international, 6, 13, 22, 23, 27, 34 ff., 44, 60, 64, 70, 80, 100, 127, 153, 155
Central Banks, 25–6, 33, 47, 69–70, 87, 124, 126–8, 140, 147, 148, 175, 181
Common Market, European, 123, 179, 184 ff.
Complacency, 113–14
Compulsory Investment-Hedging, 189 ff.
Confidence, 25, 34, 46, 48, 52, 82, 105, 169
Counterparts, 10, 14, 62, 65, 80, 86
Covering, 9, 12–13, 22, 25, 43, 60, 72–77, 79, 148
Credit inflation, 93–4
Credit squeeze, 52, 54, 63, 85, 138, 155
Cripps, Sir Stafford, 82
Cromer, Lord, 151

de Gaulle, General Charles, 39, 47, 100, 116, 177, 184, 194
Defaults, 104, 107
Defeatism, 114

Deflation, viii, 27, 45, 91, 104–5, 108, 123, 139–40, 143–5, 158–9, 161, 163, 174
Delivery dates, 97, 119–20, 131
Devaluation, vii, 1, 13, 15, 38, 42–4, 48–9, 53–5, 57–8, 60, 62, 66–8, 71, 76–7, 86–7, 104 ff., 116, 123, 126, 128, 141, 148, 154, 158 ff., 168, 174
Devaluation-prone currencies, 14, 22, 53–5, 67–8, 73, 84, 165
Discrepancies, 9, 11, 15, 92
Dividend-incomes, 21–2, 30
Dollar, vii, 3–4, 8, 12, 26, 30–1, 39–40, 54, 56, 62, 65–7, 105–8, 151, 154, 174,

Einzig, Paul, *A Dynamic Theory of Forward Exchange*, xii, 79, 147
France's Crisis, 3
A Textbook on Foreign Exchange, xii, 12
The Euro-Dollar System, 79
The History of Foreign Exchange, x
Elasticities, 162–3
Emigrants' remittances, 21
'English disease', 119–20
Equilibrium line, 15
Euro-bond market, 119, 174
Euro-currencies, 8, 13, 23, 42, 55, 75–6, 78–9, 86, 94, 104, 107–8, 127, 129, 152, 174, 178
Exchange control, 20–1, 27, 29, 42, 44, 48–52, 54, 63, 68, 76, 79, 82, 85, 86, 104, 106, 116, 123, 154 ff.
Exchange Equalisation Account, 148
Export credits, 27–8, 132
Export drives, 28, 78, 91, 123, 131 ff., 160

Flexible parities, 4, 57, 106, 169
Flight of capital, 7, 48 ff., 57, 70, 100–101, 111, 124
Floating exchange rates, 4, 57, 106, 164 ff.
Foreign debts, credits, 5, 7, 25, 34, 40–41, 111, 116, 123, 126 ff., 172
Foreign exchange brokers, 11